GRAMMAR TO GO 2

ENGLISH GRAMMAR PRACTICE

ROBERT J. DIXSON

Longman

longman.com

Grammar to Go 2
English Grammar Practice

Previously published as *Regents English Workbook 2*.

Pearson Education, 10 Bank Street, White Plains, NY 10606

Executive editor: Laura Le Dréan
Associate acquisitions editor: Dena Daniel
Development editors: Katherine Rawson, Tara Maldonado
Senior production editor: Kathleen Silloway
Production editor: Diana P. George
Marketing manager: Joe Chapple
Senior manufacturing buyer: David Dickey
Cover and interior design: Tracey Munz Cataldo
Text composition: Laserwords
Text font: MetaPlusBook 11/14

Library of Congress Cataloging-in-Publication Data

Dixson, Robert James.
   Grammar to go : English grammar practice / Robert J. Dixson.
      p. cm.
   ISBN 0-13-118283-8 (bk. 1)—ISBN 0-13-118284-6 (bk. 2)—ISBN 0-13-118285-4 (bk. 3)
   1. English language—Grammar—Problems, exercises, etc. I. Title.
   PE1112.D595 2004
   428.2'076—dc22

                                                        2004005980

ISBN: 0-13-118284-6

Printed in the United States of America
1 2 3 4 5 6 7 8 9 10—BAH—09 08 07 06 05 04

There is no need here to describe the different types of exercises that this book contains or to discuss their wide variety and extent. A glance through the following pages is enough to acquaint anyone with the book's general contents.

Since this is a workbook, there is also little to say as to how it should be used. Each exercise carries its own instructions, and the students proceed accordingly. On the other hand, there are a few points of general pedagogy that the teacher using the book should keep in mind.

First, this is a workbook, and all explanatory material has been kept to a minimum. Thus, the book is not designed to be used alone or to replace completely the regular classroom text. Rather, this book should be used to supplement the regular classroom text, to give needed variety to the lesson, or to provide additional drill materials on important points of grammar and usage.

Second, as a teacher using this book, don't assume that after students have written the answers to an exercise correctly, they know the material thoroughly and can use the principle in their everyday speech. The exercise is often only the beginning. Much drill and practice are still necessary. Therefore, ask questions or introduce simple conversation involving the particular grammar principle. Also, don't hesitate to repeat the exercises in the book several times. Run over these exercises orally in class. If the students have already written the answers in their books, they can cover these answers with their hand or with a separate sheet of paper. Continue to review past exercises that seem important to you or that have given the students difficulty.

Third, don't fall into the further error of assuming that some of the exercises in this book are too easy for your particular students. Certain exercises may seem easy to you—especially if you speak English as a native—but they still represent a real challenge to anyone learning English. With this in mind, there is one additional point of utmost importance to consider. We are not interested in tricking or even in testing the student with these exercises. That is, the exercises are not designed to find out how much a student knows or does not know. Their purpose is simply to drill the student on certain basic points of grammar and usage. The exercises are practice exercises—nothing more. For this reason, the exercises have been made as simple and as clear as possible. For the same reason, a good deal of direct repetition has been purposely introduced, not only in individual exercises but throughout the book.

There are three books in this series. *Grammar to Go 1* is for the beginning student; *Grammar to Go 2* is for the intermediate student; *Grammar to Go 3* is for the advanced student. The **Grammar to Go** series is readily adaptable to many uses and can serve effectively to supplement any standard classroom textbook. A perforated answer key at the back of the book makes classroom use or self-study equally feasible.

R.J.D.

CONTENTS

POSSESSIVE ADJECTIVES

Review

my	our	I like *my* new car.
your	your	You bought *your* house last year.
his	their	They drank *their* coffee quickly.
her		She has *her* appointment today.
its		The book lost *its* cover.

Write the correct possessive adjective in the blank.

1. Sylvia usually goes to school with _____ sister.   *her*
2. Frank likes _____ English class a lot.
3. We spent two hours on _____ homework last night.
4. Richard and Nick always do _____ homework together.
5. Mrs. Teng loves _____ children very much.
6. The dog did not eat _____ dinner.
7. _____ first name is Anna.
8. Do you always do _____ homework in the library?
9. I enjoy _____ English class very much.
10. Teresa and _____ brother study in the same class.
11. We all think a great deal of _____ English teacher.
12. Mr. Lee left _____ pen on the desk.
13. Yesterday I left _____ notebook on the bus.
14. Most parents love _____ children.
15. Both boys have on _____ new suits.
16. Mariane is wearing _____ new hat today.
17. The cat pays little attention to _____ kittens.
18. Do you always bring _____ lunch to school?
19. Miss Wong left yesterday on _____ vacation.
20. Juan writes a letter to _____ grandparents every week.
21. He asked me to help him with _____ shopping.

OBJECT PRONOUNS

Review

Subject	Object	Subject	Object
I	me	we	us
you	you	you	you
he	him	they	them
she	her		
it	it		

We use object pronouns as direct objects, indirect objects, and objects of prepositions.

> I saw *them* in London.
>
> Roger gave *me* his phone number.
>
> Susan bought the record for *him*.

Change the words in italics to the correct object pronoun.

1. I met *Suzanne* on the street yesterday. _____her_____
2. She saw *Noriko and me* in the park. _____
3. She left *her keys* in the car. _____
4. I told *the boys* about it. _____
5. I saw *you and your brother* at the movies last night. _____
6. He rode *his bicycle* to school this morning. _____
7. She told *her parents* about the accident. _____
8. I have *my book* with me. _____
9. We see *those girls* in the park every afternoon. _____
10. I liked *that movie* very much. _____
11. He sent *Nina* some flowers. _____
12. I wrote *your telephone number* in my notebook. _____
13. I eat lunch with *Henry and Charles* every day. _____
14. Put *the cat* outside. _____
15. I don't like to have *animals* in the house. _____
16. I heard *the president* on the radio last night. _____
17. You can go with *Marcia and me* to the party. _____
18. I gave the money to *my sister*. _____
19. Are you going to the movies with *Ali*? _____

myself	ourselves
yourself	yourselves
himself	themselves
herself	
itself	

Reflexive pronouns refer back to the subject of the sentence when the subject and the object are the same person.

> Henry hurt *himself* in the game.

Reflexive pronouns emphasize a person or a thing in the sentence.

> Lisa *herself* thought of the idea.

We often use the preposition *by* and a reflexive pronoun to give the meaning of "alone" or "without help."

> He prefers to do his homework *by himself*. She went to Europe *by herself*.

Write the correct reflexive pronoun in the blank.

1. Jane fell and hurt _____.   _____herself_____

2. I want to buy _____ a new hat.   _____

3. Mr. Oguri _____ will give the principal speech.   _____

4. We _____ will serve the meal.   _____

5. They all enjoyed _____ very much.   _____

6. I also enjoyed _____ very much.   _____

7. The dog hurt _____ when it jumped over the fence.   _____

8. Monique cut _____ with the knife.   _____

9. We need to look at _____ in the mirror.   _____

10. Most children like to look at _____ in the mirror.   _____

11. The president _____ will speak to the members of Congress. _____

12. I _____ will return the book to you.   _____

13. Carlos _____ saw the accident.   _____

14. Mr. Roth arranged the flowers _____.   _____

POSSESSIVE PRONOUNS

Review

mine	ours
yours	yours
his	theirs
hers	
its	

Possessive pronouns are used to avoid repeating the same words in a sentence.

That glass is *my glass*.	That glass is *mine*.
This money is *our money*.	This money is *ours*.

Change the words in italics to the correct possessive pronoun.

1. This coat is *her coat*.   <u>hers</u>
2. That car is *their car*.   _____
3. This new cell phone is *my new cell phone*.   _____
4. That car stereo is *his car stereo*.   _____
5. That dog in the yard is *our dog*.   _____
6. This desk is *his desk*.   _____
7. Those books are *your books*.   _____
8. This pencil is also *your pencil*.   _____
9. Is this magazine *her magazine*?   _____
10. Your English book is the same as *my English book*.   _____
11. Those books are *Hector and Mario's books*.   _____
12. These books are *my books and your books*.   _____
13. Both these cars are *my cars*.   _____
14. This seat is mine, and the other one is *your seat*.   _____
15. Whose pen is this? Is it *your pen*?   _____
16. Is it *Angela's coat*?   _____
17. I study in my room, and Michel studies in *his room*.   _____
18. I think this notebook is *your notebook*.   _____
19. These pencils are *their pencils*.   _____
20. I found my keys, but Tomiko couldn't find *her keys*.   _____

Most English nouns form the plural by adding *s* to the singular form.

books	friends	days

Nouns ending in *s, sh, ch, x,* or *z* add *es* to form the plural.

church → church*es*	kiss → kiss*es*	wish → wish*es*

Some nouns have irregular plurals.

child → children	man → men	person → people
foot → feet	mouse → mice	tooth → teeth
goose → geese	ox → oxen	woman → women

Write the plural form of the word.

1. lunch   _lunches_
2. tie   _____
3. class   _____
4. teacher   _____
5. beach   _____
6. window   _____
7. door   _____
8. dress   _____
9. watch   _____
10. book   _____
11. ox   _____
12. pencil   _____
13. cafeteria   _____
14. student   _____
15. wish   _____
16. headache   _____
17. box   _____
18. school   _____

19. child   _____
20. notebook   _____
21. hand   _____
22. mouse   _____
23. hat   _____
24. goose   _____
25. loss   _____
26. person   _____
27. cover   _____
28. bus   _____
29. foot   _____
30. dish   _____
31. man   _____
32. kiss   _____
33. face   _____
34. church   _____
35. cousin   _____
36. pen   _____

PLURAL OF NOUNS

Review 2

Nouns ending in *y* form their plural in two ways:

a. If a vowel precedes the *y*, add *s*.

> key ⟶ key*s*   toy ⟶ toy*s*

b. If a consonant precedes the *y*, change the *y* to *i* and add *es*.

> lady ⟶ lad*ies*   city ⟶ cit*ies*

Nouns ending in *f* or *fe* usually form their plural by changing the endings to *ves*.

> wife ⟶ wi*ves*   leaf ⟶ lea*ves*   calf ⟶ cal*ves*

Some nouns ending in *o*, where *o* is preceded by a consonant, form their plurals by adding *es*.

> hero ⟶ hero*es*   mosquito ⟶ mosquito*es*

Write the plural form of the word.

1. tomato   *tomatoes*
2. rug   _____
3. tooth   _____
4. city   _____
5. table   _____
6. knife   _____
7. fox   _____
8. potato   _____
9. pass   _____
10. boy   _____
11. street   _____
12. exercise   _____
13. echo   _____
14. copy   _____
15. wolf   _____
16. key   _____
17. sandwich   _____

18. hero   _____
19. tray   _____
20. army   _____
21. half   _____
22. thief   _____
23. leaf   _____
24. address   _____
25. curtain   _____
26. latch   _____
27. letter   _____
28. hat   _____
29. butterfly   _____
30. day   _____
31. foot   _____
32. lady   _____
33. baby   _____
34. wife   _____

Verbs in the third-person singular, present tense, follow the general spelling rules for plural nouns.

Most verbs add *s*.

> he work*s*   she drive*s*

If a verb ends in *y* preceded by a consonant, change *y* to *i* and add *es*.

> study ⟶ he stud*ies*   carry ⟶ she carr*ies*

When a verb ends in *o*, we generally add *es*.

> go ⟶ he go*es*   do ⟶ she do*es*

Verbs ending in *s*, *sh*, *ch*, *x*, or *z* take *es* endings in the third person singular.

> wish ⟶ he wish*es*   catch ⟶ she catch*es*

Change the verb to the third-person singular, present tense.

1. study   _studies_
2. like   _____
3. play   _____
4. go   _____
5. carry   _____
6. teach   _____
7. show   _____
8. do   _____
9. watch   _____
10. try   _____
11. speak   _____
12. notice   _____
13. say   _____
14. pass   _____
15. wash   _____
16. catch   _____

17. bring   _____
18. leave   _____
19. know   _____
20. think   _____
21. see   _____
22. laugh   _____
23. match   _____
24. dance   _____
25. reply   _____
26. pay   _____
27. sing   _____
28. fix   _____
29. push   _____
30. pull   _____
31. dress   _____
32. miss   _____

THIRD-PERSON SINGULAR

Review 2

Modal auxiliary verbs, such as *can, may, must, should, ought,* and *will,* do not change form in any of the three persons, singular and plural. In addition, modal auxiliaries are always followed by the simple form of the main verb. Do not add *s.*

I *can* go.	You *should* stay.	They *must* leave.

Change to the third-person singular by changing I *to* she.

1.	I know	*She knows*	23. I must see	_____
2.	I can speak	*She can speak*	24. I pass	_____
3.	I must go	_____	25. I will take	_____
4.	I fix	_____	26. I teach	_____
5.	I have	_____	27. I may work	_____
6.	I will see	_____	28. I work	_____
7.	I may study	_____	29. I want	_____
8.	I live	_____	30. I do	_____
9.	I study	_____	31. I wish	_____
10.	I will be	_____	32. I can meet	_____
11.	I can go	_____	33. I try	_____
12.	I should study	_____	34. I leave	_____
13.	I play	_____	35. I use	_____
14.	I carry	_____	36. I wash	_____
15.	I go	_____	37. I sing	_____
16.	I should go	_____	38. I will know	_____
17.	I can wait	_____	39. I must try	_____
18.	I wait	_____	40. I reply	_____
19.	I enjoy	_____	41. I will try	_____
20.	I will enjoy	_____	42. I should see	_____
21.	I watch	_____	43. I must have	_____
22.	I like	_____	44. I will fix	_____

Write the correct form of the simple present tense of the verb in parentheses.

1. Yuriko (like) to study English.   *likes*

2. Pauline (have) many friends in this school. _____

3. We (study) in the same class. _____

4. Kenji also (study) in our class. _____

5. Yoko and I (work) at the same office. _____

6. Both of our English teachers (come) from Canada. _____

7. They (explain) things very clearly. _____

8. Mr. Silva (teach) this class. _____

9. I (watch) TV every night. _____

10. My father (listen) to music every night. _____

11. The children (play) in the park every afternoon. _____

12. They (live) on this street. _____

13. Juanita (live) on Church Street. _____

14. Alma (go) to the movies almost every night. _____

15. We always (come) to school by bus. _____

16. Peter (do) his homework very carefully. _____

17. He never (make) mistakes in spelling. _____

18. You (speak) English very well. _____

19. We both (want) to learn English well. _____

20. They (have) work to do today. _____

21. Nadia (have) two cars. _____

22. Hong (play) tennis every weekend. _____

23. Mrs. Kim generally (go) to the United States in the summer. _____

24. She sometimes (stay) there for a whole month. _____

25. At the carnival, you (spin) the wheel to win a prize. _____

26. It (begin) to get cold in October. _____

SUBJECT-VERB AGREEMENT

Review

Change the word in italics to the plural form. Make the corresponding change in the verb. Write the subject and the verb in the blank.

1. The *book* is on the table.   _The books are_
2. *This* is mine. _____
3. *I* am busy today. _____
4. *She* likes to study English. _____
5. *That book* belongs to William. _____
6. *He* was afraid of the dog. _____
7. The *boy* does the work well. _____
8. *He* is writing the exercises. _____
9. The *child* is afraid of the dog. _____
10. *This pencil* belongs to Mary. _____
11. The *tomato* is ripe. _____
12. The *dish* is on the table. _____
13. The *class* has started. _____
14. The *woman* is waiting outside. _____
15. *This book* is yours. _____
16. *I* am going to study French. _____
17. *She* is making good progress. _____
18. The *bus* is late today. _____
19. The *man* has left. _____
20. *He* will leave soon. _____
21. *She* can speak English well. _____
22. The *boy* must study more. _____
23. *She* was here yesterday. _____
24. The *leaf* is falling from the tree. _____
25. The *wife* of Henry VIII was not happy. _____
26. The *person* has gone away. _____

Write the opposite of the word.

1.	young	*old*	25.	clean	_____
2.	high	_____	26.	absent	_____
3.	arrive	_____	27.	beautiful	_____
4.	inside	_____	28.	happy	_____
5.	wild	_____	29.	easy	_____
6.	awake	_____	30.	narrow	_____
7.	brave	_____	31.	lose	_____
8.	hard	_____	32.	low	_____
9.	sharp	_____	33.	under	_____
10.	smooth	_____	34.	east	_____
11.	borrow	_____	35.	north	_____
12.	forward	_____	36.	late	_____
13.	polite	_____	37.	buy	_____
14.	thick	_____	38.	tall	_____
15.	before	_____	39.	often	_____
16.	in front of	_____	40.	sweet	_____
17.	expensive	_____	41.	cause	_____
18.	dry	_____	42.	good	_____
19.	false	_____	43.	summer	_____
20.	child	_____	44.	big	_____
21.	empty	_____	45.	find	_____
22.	push	_____	46.	remember	_____
23.	wide	_____	47.	future	_____
24.	loose	_____	48.	best	_____

PREPOSITIONS 1

Write the correct preposition in the blank.

1. I explained the matter _____ her very clearly.   _____ *to* _____

2. What is the matter _____ him?   _____

3. She seems to be _____ a big hurry.   _____

4. We went there _____ mistake.   _____

5. What has happened _____ Ted?   _____

6. This is an exception _____ the rule.   _____

7. He was absent _____ class twice last week.   _____

8. She should return _____ her book soon.   _____

9. This river is one of the longest _____ the world.   _____

10. They plan to take a trip _____ the world.   _____

11. He says that he'll be back _____ a few minutes.   _____

12. The police officer looked _____ me suspiciously.   _____

13. Angela is looking _____ the book that she lost.   _____

14. How many new words do you look up _____ your
dictionary every day?   _____

15. They may stay in Brazil _____ several months.   _____

16. I plan to go to San Francisco _____ plane.   _____

17. He arrived _____ school twenty minutes late.   _____

18. I do not know the first thing _____ mathematics.   _____

19. She copied her speech word _____ word from
the encyclopedia.   _____

20. Be sure to write the report _____ the computer.   _____

21. His face is familiar _____ me.   _____

22. Don't mention anything about it _____ him.   _____

23. Let's sit here on this bench _____ a while.   _____

24. She paid _____ credit card.   _____

Select the correct form. Write your answer in the blank.

1. The weather today is warmer (than, as) it was yesterday. _____*than*_____

2. Listen! The water (is running, runs). _____

3. They (have lived, lived) there since January. _____

4. We (was, were) both absent from class yesterday. _____

5. My friend sent (me, to me) a present from Singapore. _____

6. They (have, are having) their lunch now. _____

7. How (much, many) coffee do you want? _____

8. Please give (me, my) that book. _____

9. I didn't hear (someone, anyone) in the room. _____

10. He (works, has worked) for that company for many years. _____

11. He always (is coming, comes) to school by bus. _____

12. I spoke to him (on, by) the telephone yesterday. _____

13. What time did you (get, got) up this morning? _____

14. I (wrote, have written) a letter to him yesterday. _____

15. Rose told (us, to us) about her trip to Africa. _____

16. Ana and Pablo (wants, want) me to eat dinner with them tonight. _____

17. It is not difficult (learn, to learn) English. _____

18. Sam doesn't (live, lives) near here. _____

19. (This, These) pencils belong to Giorgio. _____

20. He is (a, an) honest man. _____

21. Sue (has, have) many friends in this school. _____

22. How many students (is there, are there) in your English class? _____

23. My parents painted the house (ourselves, themselves). _____

24. Her book is here. (His, Him) is over there. _____

REGULAR VERBS, PAST TENSE

Review

The past tense of regular verbs is formed by adding *ed* to their singular form.

> work ⟶ work*ed*   play ⟶ play*ed*

If the verb ends in *e*, only *d* is added.

> change ⟶ change*d*   close ⟶ close*d*

If the verb ends in *y*, preceded by a consonant, change the *y* to *i* and add *ed*.

> study ⟶ stud*ied*   marry ⟶ marr*ied*

If a single final consonant follows a single stressed vowel, double the final consonant before adding *ed*.

> plan ⟶ plan*ned*   admit ⟶ admit*ted*

Write the past tense form of the verb.

1.	describe	*described*	17.	seem
2.	force		18.	enjoy
3.	study		19.	appear
4.	indicate		20.	notice
5.	need		21.	travel
6.	learn		22.	please
7.	practice		23.	spell
8.	use		24.	face
9.	marry		25.	worry
10.	manage		26.	depend
11.	carry		27.	decrease
12.	play		28.	hop
13.	guide		29.	point
14.	stop		30.	suppose
15.	hope		31.	refer
16.	cry		32.	insist

In regular verbs ending in *t* or *d*, the *ed* is pronounced as a separate syllable.

> count ⟶ count(ed)　　wait ⟶ wait(ed)　　land ⟶ land(ed)

When we add *ed* to regular verbs of one syllable not ending in *t* or *d*, they are pronounced as one syllable.

> live ⟶ lived　　close ⟶ closed　　cross ⟶ crossed

Pronounce the following past tense forms. If the word is pronounced as one syllable, write the number 1 in the blank. If it is pronounced as two syllables, write 2 in the blank.

1.	ended	2	21.	rushed	___
2.	watched	1	22.	parted	___
3.	counted	___	23.	cooked	___
4.	stayed	___	24.	rented	___
5.	needed	___	25.	lived	___
6.	called	___	26.	shared	___
7.	seemed	___	27.	lasted	___
8.	planned	___	28.	closed	___
9.	waited	___	29.	helped	___
10.	washed	___	30.	landed	___
11.	wanted	___	31.	used	___
12.	walked	___	32.	hoped	___
13.	pushed	___	33.	handed	___
14.	spelled	___	34.	crossed	___
15.	planted	___	35.	signed	___
16.	cleaned	___	36.	earned	___
17.	asked	___	37.	painted	___
18.	pointed	___	38.	dropped	___
19.	moved	___	39.	burned	___
20.	shopped	___	40.	laughed	___

IRREGULAR VERBS, PAST TENSE

Review 1

Review the forms of these irregular verbs. Remember that the past tense form is the same as the past participle form for these verbs.

bring → brought	feel → felt	mean → meant
buy → bought	keep → kept	sleep → slept
catch → caught	kneel → knelt	sweep → swept
creep → crept	leave → left	teach → taught
deal → dealt	lose → lost	think → thought

Write the past tense form of the verb in parentheses. Practice reading the sentences in the past tense.

1. I (sleep) more than ten hours last night.   *slept*

2. He (buy) that car last year. _____

3. Rob (lose) the game at the tournament yesterday. _____

4. It was after ten o'clock when she (leave). _____

5. I didn't understand what he (mean). _____

6. The police (catch) the thief last night after a long search. _____

7. Sandra (bring) her little brother to class yesterday. _____

8. They (sweep) each of the rooms carefully. _____

9. The president's speech (deal) with the subject of taxes. _____

10. Mike (teach) us English last semester. _____

11. I (think) I could not come to the lesson today. _____

12. When Annette won the prize, her family naturally (feel) very proud of her. _____

13. The dog put his tail between his legs and (creep) out of the room. _____

14. The teacher asked them to stop, but the two boys (keep) on talking. _____

15. She (kneel) down to pick up a coin. _____

16. I (leave) my cell phone on the bus. _____

17. I (mean) to call you yesterday, but I forgot. _____

18. Although we did not arrive until late, our hosts (keep) dinner hot for us. _____

19. I (buy) this hat in London. _____

Review the forms of these irregular verbs. Remember that the past tense form is the same as the past participle form for these verbs. They form the past tense by changing the vowel sound.

dig → dug	hold → held	shoot → shot
feed → fed	lead → led	sit → sat
fight → fought	meet → met	stand → stood
find → found	read → read	strike → struck
hang → hung	shine → shone	win → won

Hang has another past tense form, *hanged*, used only in reference to death by hanging. *Shine* also has another past tense form, *shined*. Thus, "The sun *shone*," but "John *shined* his shoes."

Write the past tense form of the verb in parentheses. Practice reading the sentences in the past tense.

1. Our team (win) both games last week.   _____won_____

2. I (find) this book on the bus yesterday.   _____

3. I (meet) him several years ago in Washington.   _____

4. Last year the senior class (hold) its banquet at the Springhouse Inn.   _____

5. We (sit) in the first row at the theater last evening.   _____

6. The lightning (strike) two houses on our block last week.   _____

7. I (read) about the accident in yesterday's newspaper.   _____

8. The police worked on the case for several months before they
   finally (find) the thief.   _____

9. The guide (lead) us down one long hall after another.   _____

10. Dick (hang) up his hat and coat as soon as he came in.   _____

11. Our troops (fight) well, but the enemy was too strong.   _____

12. We (hold) the meeting in the school auditorium.   _____

13. The dog (dig) up two old bones.   _____

14. The sun (shine) all day yesterday.   _____

15. They (feed) the guests an excellent meal.   _____

NEGATIVE FORM

Review 1

The negative of *to be*, in both present and past tenses, is formed by placing *not* after the verb. The contracted forms are generally used.

> He *is not (isn't)* a good tennis player.   She *was not (wasn't)* at our party last night.
>
> They *are not (aren't)* good tennis players.   They *were not (weren't)* at our party last night.

Change the sentence to the negative form. Use contractions.

1. Joe is in our class.   _____ *isn't* _____
2. You are listening to me.   _____ *aren't listening* _____
3. She is very tired now.   _____
4. He is very busy today.   _____
5. They were here yesterday.   _____
6. He is studying in our group.   _____
7. She is talking on the phone right now.   _____
8. The children are very hungry now.   _____
9. She is a good French speaker.   _____
10. We are going to the movies tonight.   _____
11. They are old friends.   _____
12. She is a good cook.   _____
13. He was in Chicago last week.   _____
14. They were at the office yesterday.   _____
15. We were tired after the dance.   _____
16. I am a computer expert.   _____
17. There is enough sugar in the bowl.   _____
18. There were many students absent last night.   _____
19. We are going to be late for class.   _____
20. They are working on the computer.   _____
21. He is standing outside.   _____

Form the negative of sentences with modal auxiliary verbs (*can, must, may, will, should,* etc.) by placing *not* after the modal auxiliary.

> You *should not (shouldn't)* break a promise.   We *will not (won't)* go by boat this year.

The contracted forms *can't, shouldn't, won't,* and *mustn't* are generally used. *May not* and *might not* are not contracted.

Change the sentence to the negative form. Use contractions whenever possible.

1. Joe will study in our group.   *won't study*

2. You must tell him about it.   _____

3. She may return later.   _____

4. It might rain tonight.   _____

5. I can understand TV programs in English.   _____

6. We may leave class early today.   _____

7. She should spend more time on that report.   _____

8. They will be back at five o'clock.   _____

9. She can speak French well.   _____

10. You might enjoy this movie.   _____

11. We can have dinner with you tonight.   _____

12. She can cook Chinese food.   _____

13. He will go to Chicago next Monday.   _____

14. She will call you tonight.   _____

15. We might be tired after the dance.   _____

16. You may use a dictionary during the test.   _____

17. They might ask for help.   _____

18. There will be a test next week.   _____

19. I can meet you later.   _____

20. You must type your report on the computer.   _____

21. You may park here.   _____

NEGATIVE FORM

Review 3

The auxiliaries *do* and *does* + *not* are used to form negative sentences in the present tense. Place *do not* or *does not* before the simple form of the verb.

I speak French well.	I *do not (don't)* speak French well.
She works hard at the office.	She *does not (doesn't)* work hard at the office.

To form the negative in the past tense, place *did not* before the simple form of the verb. *Did* is used for all persons, singular and plural.

He came to class early.	He *did not (didn't)* come to class early.
We ate a big lunch at noon.	We *did not (didn't)* eat a big lunch at noon.

The contracted forms are generally used.

Change the sentence to the negative form. Use contractions whenever possible.

1. She comes to class on time.   _____ *doesn't come* _____
2. They live near here.   _____
3. I know him very well.   _____
4. I ate two rolls this morning.   _____
5. We want to learn French.   _____
6. The bus stopped on this corner.   _____
7. We cooked dinner at home last night.   _____
8. She sat near me in class.   _____
9. He reads a lot of books in French.   _____
10. He speaks to us in English.   _____
11. Tim eats too much.   _____
12. She came with me to the lesson.   _____
13. I had a lot of work to do yesterday.   _____
14. The children drank all the milk.   _____
15. Teresa watched the game on TV last night.   _____
16. He hung his coat on the chair.   _____
17. I found my book.   _____
18. We sit in the first row in class.   _____
19. We learned a lot of new words yesterday.   _____
20. They held the meeting in the school auditorium.   _____

Change the sentence to the negative form. Use contractions whenever possible.

1. He will return next week.   *won't return*
2. He speaks English well.   _____
3. It is raining hard.   _____
4. She is a good student.   _____
5. We were late for the lesson this morning.   _____
6. I met Giselle on Fifth Avenue yesterday.   _____
7. Our team won both games.   _____
8. He will be on time this evening.   _____
9. She came to class late this morning.   _____
10. Adela feels much better today.   _____
11. The movie last night was very good.   _____
12. They are going to Spain next year.   _____
13. She can speak Japanese well.   _____
14. You should park here.   _____
15. Felipe should spend more time on his homework.   _____
16. They go to the movies every night.   _____
17. I like Italian movies.   _____
18. She is a good teacher.   _____
19. He will tell you the truth.   _____
20. He called me last night.   _____
21. She is wearing a brown sweater.   _____
22. The train left at four o'clock.   _____
23. I understand him very well.   _____
24. He speaks very slowly.   _____
25. I was sleeping at that time.   _____
26. We went to the movies at seven o'clock.   _____
27. He has seen this Web site many times.   _____

QUESTION FORM

Review 1

To form questions with *to be* in the present and past tenses, place *to be* before the subject.

Is Lisa the best student in your class?	***Were your friends*** on time yesterday?

Remember that in *there + be* sentences, *there* is treated like a subject.

Change the sentence to the question form. Write the verb and subject in the blank.

1. Sam is in our class.   _Is Sam_____

2. He is a good French speaker. _____

3. She is a politician. _____

4. George was at home yesterday. _____

5. They were tired after the dance. _____

6. She is a good manager. _____

7. Lily is on vacation. _____

8. Mr. and Mrs. Kim are in Chicago this week. _____

9. They are angry. _____

10. She is studying to be a lawyer. _____

11. Anil is playing tennis this afternoon. _____

12. They are making a phone call. _____

13. He is an excellent student. _____

14. There were two men in the office. _____

15. He was hungry before dinner. _____

16. They were good friends. _____

17. They were both here yesterday. _____

18. It is raining hard. _____

19. They are going to a meeting. _____

20. You were here yesterday. _____

21. There is no time to discuss it. _____

22. We were almost home when the car broke down. _____

23. They were arguing for hours. _____

Form questions with modal auxiliaries (*can, may, will, should,* etc.) by placing the modal auxiliary before the subject.

> ***May we* leave early today?   *Will you* have time to finish before dinner?**

Change the sentence to the question form. Write the verb and subject in the blank.

1. Sam will study in our group. — *Will Sam study*
2. She can speak French well. — _____
3. She should study harder. — _____
4. He may sit here. — _____
5. They will be tired after the dance. — _____
6. She can run the office well. — _____
7. He can go with us to the movies. — _____
8. He should mention it to her. — _____
9. They will be angry. — _____
10. She should study to be a lawyer. — _____
11. Mr. Darbari will go to Chicago next week. — _____
12. She will call us later. — _____
13. He should drink less coffee. — _____
14. We can use this computer. — _____
15. He should study more. — _____
16. They will become friends. — _____
17. We may leave class early today. — _____
18. It will rain all weekend. — _____
19. We may sit in the garden. — _____
20. She will be ready soon. — _____
21. Our friends should arrive soon. — _____
22. This file must stay in the office. — _____
23. She can go with you. — _____

Review 3

Form questions in the simple present tense by placing the auxiliary *do* before the subject. Use *does* for the third person singular.

> ***Do we** have enough gas to get home?*   ***Does Andy** work in your office?*

Form questions in the past tense by placing the auxiliary *did* before the subject.

> ***Did Judy** drive there by herself?*   ***Did you** enjoy your holiday in Greece?*

Do, does, and *did* are always followed by the simple form of the verb.

Change the sentence to the question form. Write the auxiliary, followed by the subject and the main verb, in the blank.

1. She comes to class on time.   *Does she come*
2. They left at two o'clock.   _____
3. She studies in the library.   _____
4. He bought a new car last year.   _____
5. She drives her brother to class.   _____
6. Daniela answered the phone.   _____
7. He sat in the first row.   _____
8. He speaks English very clearly.   _____
9. They go to the movies almost every night.   _____
10. They met in Athens last year.   _____
11. Billy cut his finger badly.   _____
12. She gave us some good advice.   _____
13. They live on the second floor.   _____
14. You drink water with your meals.   _____
15. The bus comes every half hour.   _____
16. The train arrived on time.   _____
17. He writes her every week.   _____
18. They brought Steve a present from New York.   _____
19. He lost his money in Monte Carlo.   _____
20. They caught the thief after a long search.   _____

To form questions with question words, such as *what, where, why,* and *when,* place the question word in front of the question.

Are they hungry?	*Why* are they hungry?
Does she study?	*What* does she study?
Did he leave?	*When* did he leave?
Can you sing?	*What* can you sing?

Change the sentence to the question form using the question words in parentheses. Use pronouns in your questions.

1. She went somewhere by plane. (Where)   _Where did she go?_
2. He will be here soon. (When) _____
3. The children are very tired. (Why) _____
4. He works many hours a day. (How many hours) _____
5. The boys spent a long time in the park. (How long) _____
6. Paula lives nearby. (Where) _____
7. Mary can have dinner at our house. (When) _____
8. The telephone rang late last night. (What time) _____
9. He is walking fast. (Why) _____
10. We need more coffee. (How much) _____
11. Antonia will tell us all about it. (When) _____
12. The train left late. (What time) _____
13. It rained for a long time last night. (How long) _____
14. The plane will arrive in Philadelphia early. (What time) _____
15. You should hang up your coat. (Where) _____
16. The baby is crying. (Why) _____
17. They forgot the gift at home. (What) _____
18. Ryan invited the girls to the party. (Where) _____
19. They have ten children. (How many) _____
20. She can visit us next summer. (When) _____

The is a definite article. It refers to a particular object or to particular objects.

> **The book that I bought is on *the* table.   *The* pictures you took are excellent.**

Nouns that name an indefinite quantity or an intangible quality do not take an article.

> **Gold is a precious metal.   Honesty is always appreciated.**

When these nouns are used to express a particular quality or quantity, they should be preceded by *the*.

> **The gold in this jewelry is very old.   The honesty of that child is above question.**

The is not used before the names of persons, countries, continents, streets, cities, or towns when they are used as proper nouns. (Exceptions: *the* United States, *the* Dominican Republic, etc.)

> **Ms. Torrence lives on White Oak Lane, in Fairfax. She's going to travel to Europe next summer. She'll visit London, Paris, and Rome.**

When these words are used as adjectives, they are preceded by *the*.

> **London is a large city.   The London transportation system is excellent.**

Write the article the, *if necessary, in the blank. If it is not necessary, leave blank.*

1. He came here directly from _____ Mexico.   _(no article)_

2. They say that _____ weather in Acapulco is beautiful.   _the_

3. Mr. and Mrs. Bielski are now traveling in _____ Brazil.   _____

4. He has always lived in _____ United States.   _____

5. Does Maria speak _____ English well?   _____

6. _____ English language is not difficult to learn.   _____

7. I like _____ tea better than coffee.   _____

8. _____ tea in your cup is Japanese.   _____

9. _____ women are important in U.S. politics.   _____

10. Do you agree that _____ dogs make nice pets?   _____

11. We all took a walk along _____ Fifth Avenue.   _____

The simple present tense is used to describe an action that happens regularly or in general.

> It always *rains* in April here.   They *eat* dinner around eight o'clock.

The present continuous tense describes an action which is occurring at the moment of speaking.

> I *am typing* this document. (now)   We *are having* trouble with the computer.

Write the present continuous or the simple present tense of the verb in parentheses.

1. Your phone (ring) a lot. _____*rings*_____

2. Your phone (ring) now. _____

3. She (write) a lot of letters to her parents. _____

4. Alice is busy now. She (write) a letter. _____

5. Mr. Sato (read) all the time. _____

6. He (read) more than two books every week. _____

7. Look! He (read) a book now. _____

8. It (rain) a great deal during the spring months. _____

9. Look! It (begin) to rain. _____

10. Listen! Someone (knock) at the door. _____

11. The bus always (stop) at this corner. _____

12. The bus (stop) for us now. _____

13. I always (get) on the bus at this corner. _____

14. Mr. and Mrs. Gonzalez (build) a new home on Second Avenue. _____

15. We (have) English lessons three times a week. _____

16. We (have) our English lesson now. _____

17. Look! Rose (wave) to us from across the street. _____

18. Patricia always (come) to school by bus. _____

19. Be quiet or you will wake the baby. She (sleep). _____

20. She (sleep) about fourteen hours a day. _____

Form the past continuous tense with the past tense of *to be* and the present participle of the main verb.

I was working.	We were working.
You were working.	You were working.
He was working.	They were working.
She was working.	
It was working.	

The past continuous is used to describe an action that was going on when another action took place.

I *was sleeping* when you phoned.

We *were leaving* the house when they arrived.

Write the past continuous tense of the verb in parentheses.

1. I (sleep) when the phone rang. _____was sleeping_____

2. We (sit) in the park when it began to rain. _____

3. The sun (shine) brightly when I got up this morning. _____

4. I (walk) down the street when I met him. _____

5. We (have) lunch when she called. _____

6. Bruce (study) when I went to see him last night. _____

7. He fell while he (play) in the park. _____

8. They (drive) to Chicago when the accident happened. _____

9. The teacher (write) on the board when we entered the classroom. _____

10. She fell while she (get) off the bus. _____

11. My mother (prepare) dinner when I got home. _____

12. It (rain) hard when I left home. _____

13. When I arrived at school, the sun (shine). _____

14. Molly (talk) with Jack when I passed them in the hall. _____

15. They (watch) TV when we called them. _____

16. I (cook) dinner when the doorbell rang. _____

17. Both children (sleep) when I went into the room. _____

18. The man (suffer) greatly when the ambulance arrived. _____

Write the simple past or past continuous tense of the verb in parentheses.

1. I (sleep) well last night.

    slept

2. I (sleep) when the fire started.

    _____

3. When I got up this morning, the wind (blow) hard.

    _____

4. It (rain) hard last night.

    _____

5. It (rain) hard when I left home.

    _____

6. Susie fell while she (play) in the park.

    _____

7. She (play) in the park all afternoon.

    _____

8. We (have) dinner when you called.

    _____

9. I (read) two new books last week.

    _____

10. When we got there, Keith (read) the newspaper.

    _____

11. I (write) several letters last night.

    _____

12. I (write) a letter when you called me.

    _____

13. The sun (shine) brightly when I got up this morning.

    _____

14. The telephone (ring) just as I was leaving.

    _____

15. Mr. Ryan (drive) to Chicago in his new car.

    _____

16. The accident happened while he (drive) to Chicago.

    _____

17. The boys (play) baseball all afternoon yesterday.

    _____

18. Pedro fell and hurt himself while he (play) baseball.

    _____

19. We (see) Josie at the movie theater last night.

    _____

20. We met Yuriko just as she (leave) school.

    _____

21. We (wait) an hour for you after class yesterday.

    _____

22. While we (wait) for a taxi, Martha came along and took us home.

    _____

23. He (paint) the house last summer.

    _____

24. He (paint) when he fell off the ladder.

    _____

25. She (go) to the store already.

    _____

26. She (go) to the store when it began to rain.

    _____

Write the correct preposition in the blank.

1. We arrived _____ Miami at exactly six o'clock.   *in*

2. They live _____ Washington Avenue.   _____

3. He arrived _____ school at nine o'clock.   _____

4. They live across the street _____ us.   _____

5. He listens _____ the radio every night.   _____

6. We stayed _____ the Hotel Roma.   _____

7. She refused to shake hands _____ him.   _____

8. They are going to New York _____ plane.   _____

9. The plane flew directly _____ our house.   _____

10. She placed her coat _____ top of mine.   _____

11. The senator spoke _____ the faculty.   _____

12. There is something wrong _____ this computer.   _____

13. I spoke to him _____ the telephone last night.   _____

14. I'll call you back _____ twenty minutes.   _____

15. We waited for you _____ an hour.   _____

16. I'll be back _____ ten minutes.   _____

17. They weren't _____ the hotel last night.   _____

18. I am going to Bonnie's house _____ dinner.   _____

19. He is going to ask her _____ a date.   _____

20. What are your plans _____ the weekend?   _____

21. Anne will tell you all _____ our plans.   _____

22. The man died _____ a heart attack.   _____

23. What is the matter _____ John today?   _____

24. He should be more careful _____ his health.   _____

25. She lives far _____ here.   _____

Select the correct answer and write it in the blank.

1. They came to class earlier (than, as) we.   *than*
2. "Where (do, did) you live now?" she asked.   _____
3. There (was, were) many students absent from class.   _____
4. He is (a, an) athlete.   _____
5. The last lesson was (a, an) easy one.   _____
6. (This, These) books belong to my brother.   _____
7. These books are (my, mine).   _____
8. Ling and her brother (were, was) sick last week.   _____
9. Does Ms. Eng (eat, eats) very much?   _____
10. Listen! The stereo (plays, is playing).   _____
11. He has lived in that same house (since, for) many years.   _____
12. I (saw, have seen) that movie last week.   _____
13. When I arrived, they (ate, were eating).   _____
14. Penny always (comes, is coming) to school by bus.   _____
15. He sent (her, to her) a beautiful bouquet of flowers.   _____
16. Look! Carmen (rides, is riding) her bicycle.   _____
17. It (rained, was raining) hard when I got up this morning.   _____
18. He (works, has worked) for that firm since January.   _____
19. Ivan (has, have) two cars.   _____
20. He will (buys, buy) another car.   _____
21. We (was, were) all late for the meeting.   _____
22. He (study, studies) at our school.   _____
23. They (take, are taking) a test.   _____
24. The boys (was, were) out all night.   _____
25. Gladys and Sylvia (is, are) planning a trip.   _____

HAVE TO

Present Tense

Must and *have to* express obligation or need. We use *have to* more often than *must*.

> You *must* study for this exam. You *have to* study for this exam.
>
> Harry *must* leave town on business. Harry *has to* leave town on business.

Change the words in italics to the correct form of have to + *verb.*

1. They *must prepare* their exercises more carefully. _____have to prepare_____

2. She *must go* to Chicago tonight. _____

3. She *must leave* at once. _____

4. I *must be* there before four o'clock. _____

5. We *must learn* at least ten new words every day. _____

6. I *must have* more spending money. _____

7. Everyone *must work* eight hours a day. _____

8. He *must go* to the hospital to see his friend. _____

9. You *must wait* in the reception area. _____

10. I *must go* to the bank. _____

11. He *must spend* more time on his homework. _____

12. I *must go* to the dentist. _____

13. He *must be* in his office before nine o'clock. _____

14. We *must leave* before Hugh gets here. _____

15. You *must write* your answers in the book. _____

16. Everyone *must write* a composition for tomorrow's class. _____

17. They *must remain* there all afternoon. _____

18. I *must get* there before three o'clock. _____

19. She *must stay* in bed for at least three weeks. _____

20. After that, she *must visit* the doctor every week. _____

21. On Wednesday, I *must meet* with my son's teacher. _____

22. Tomorrow, we *must finish* this exercise. _____

23. She *must watch* her little sister. _____

Past, Future, and Present Perfect

Must has no past or future tenses. We use *have to* to express obligation or need in the past, future, or present perfect tenses.

> I *have to* leave early tonight.
>
> I *had to* leave early last night.
>
> I'*ll have to* leave early tomorrow.
>
> I *have had to* leave early every day this week.

A. *Change the sentence to the past tense.*

1. I have to write a lot of letters.   _____ had to write _____

2. He has to leave for school at eight o'clock. _____

3. She has to work very hard. _____

4. They have to get up early every morning. _____

5. We have to walk to school. _____

6. I have to have more money. _____

B. *Change the sentence to the future tense.*

1. He has to work very hard.   _____ will have to work _____

2. You have to return later. _____

3. We have to do this next week. _____

4. She has to be there before nine o'clock. _____

5. I have to buy the tickets first. _____

6. We have to wait at least an hour for him. _____

C. *Change the sentence to the present perfect tense.*

1. We have to ask for help several times.   _____ have had to ask _____

2. Peter has to learn to drive. _____

3. You have to go on a diet. _____

4. They have to return from their vacation early. _____

5. I have to call them three times. _____

6. Angela has to cook all day. _____

7. You have to study every night this week. _____

Negative Form

To form the negative with *have to*, place *do not*, *does not*, *did not*, or *will not* before *have*. The contracted forms *don't*, *doesn't*, *didn't*, and *won't* are normally used.

I have to catch the seven-thirty train.	I *don't have to* catch the seven-thirty train.
Lisa will have to stay with you.	Lisa *won't have to* stay with you.
They had to help me.	They *didn't have to* help me.

Change the sentence to the negative form. Use contractions.

1. She has to work late tonight.   *doesn't have to work*

2. He had to leave early.   _____

3. We have to study hard for our next exam.   _____

4. I have to write that letter at once.   _____

5. I had to wait a long time to see him.   _____

6. She has to spend more time on her homework.   _____

7. I have to return later.   _____

8. He has to be at his office before eight o'clock.   _____

9. They have to leave before Wednesday.   _____

10. We had to walk to school.   _____

11. You will have to send him a telegram.   _____

12. You have to wait for me.   _____

13. We had to pay the doctor for her services.   _____

14. I had to go to the bank.   _____

15. I have to cash his check today.   _____

16. We will have to invite Mary to the party.   _____

17. She has to take an exam in English.   _____

18. He had to join the navy.   _____

19. She has to leave for Mexico this week.   _____

20. We have to write a composition every week.   _____

21. We had to write a letter to the lawyer.   _____

To form questions with *have to*, place *do*, *does*, *did*, or *will* before the subject.

Sally has to play in a tennis match.	*Does* Sally have to play in a tennis match?
We will have to be ready early.	*Will* we have to be ready early?

Change the sentence to the question form.

1. John has to stay home tonight.   _____Does John have to stay_____
2. He had to stay home last night, too.   _____
3. The students have to learn many new words.   _____
4. They will have to write a composition each week.   _____
5. She had to wait for him for an hour.   _____
6. You have to return later.   _____
7. She had to go to the doctor.   _____
8. She has to take another exam.   _____
9. We had to invite Eric to the party.   _____
10. He has to leave for Europe next week.   _____
11. We will have to write our exercises carefully.   _____
12. They have to arrive at school before nine o'clock.   _____
13. Tom has to get up early every morning.   _____
14. Sue has to help her mother.   _____
15. She had to prepare the dinner.   _____
16. She has to work very hard.   _____
17. They had to stay home last night and study.   _____
18. He has to go to the hospital for an operation.   _____
19. I have to sign my name at the bottom of the page.   _____
20. We had to send him an e-mail.   _____

Say is used in direct quotations.

> Joseph *said*, "It's too early to leave for the theater."
>
> She *said* to me, "Your computer print-out is ready."

Say is used for indirect quotations where the person to whom the words are spoken is not mentioned.

> Harvey *said* that he could not come tomorrow.

Tell is used for indirect quotations when the person to whom the words are spoken is mentioned.

> Harvey *told me* that he could not come tomorrow.

Tell is used in the following expressions: *to tell the truth, to tell a lie, to tell a story, to tell time, to tell a secret, to tell about something.*

The word *that*, when used to introduce a subordinate clause as in these sentences, is often dropped in everyday speech. We may say, *"She said that she was busy"* or *"She said she was busy."* Both forms are correct.

Write the correct form of say *or* tell *in the blank.*

1. She _____ both of us that she was going to get married.   *told*

2. Roger _____ he was busy after class.   _____

3. He _____ that he always ate lunch in the cafeteria.   _____

4. Sally always _____ the truth.   _____

5. I _____ you the car belonged to George.   _____

6. Susan _____ that she could teach me to paint.   _____

7. Robert _____, "The book is from the library."   _____

8. She _____ me a big secret.   _____

9. "I'm sorry I was late," he _____.   _____

10. Dolores _____ that she felt ill.   _____

11. I _____ the teacher that I already knew how to type.   _____

12. He _____ me that Marc was in the hospital.   _____

13. Annette likes to _____ stories about her travels.   _____

> I have worked.   We have worked.
>
> You have worked.   You have worked.
>
> He has worked.   They have worked.
>
> She has worked.
>
> It has worked.

The present perfect tense is for an action that began in the past and is still continuing.

> She *has owned* her house since 1984. (She still owns it.)
>
> We *have known* Bill for years. (We know him now.)

Remember that the simple past tense describes an action that happened at a definite time in the past.

> We *went* there last year.

Write the simple past or present perfect tense of the verb in parentheses.

1. We (live) in this house for almost five years.   _*have lived*_

2. From 1992 to 2002, we (live) on 96th Street.   _____

3. Marie-France (begin) to study English as soon as she arrived in the United States.   _____

4. She (study) English continuously since then.   _____

5. Ricardo (study) French when he was in high school.   _____

6. The First World War (begin) in 1914 and ended in 1918.   _____

7. We (be) in California last winter.   _____

8. They (live) in California since 1994.   _____

9. My last job was in Chicago. I (work) there for four years.   _____

10. My present job is in New York. I (work) here for two years.   _____

11. Sonia and I are good friends. In fact, we (be) good friends for more than ten years.   _____

12. We (become) friends when we were students in the university.   _____

13. Dr. Pavlik (be) our family doctor ever since we moved to this town.   _____

ABBREVIATIONS

Write the full form of the abbreviations.

1. 6 oz.   *six ounces*
2. 1 lb.   _____
3. 1 mi.   _____
4. 7 A.M.   _____
5. 6 P.M.   _____
6. .5   _____
7. 1/2   _____
8. 1/4   _____
9. 6%   _____
10. #5   _____
11. 68°   _____
12. AC   _____
13. DC   _____
14. etc.   _____
15. 1 gal. _____
16. TV   _____
17. qt.   _____
18. pt.   _____
19. yd.   _____
20. in.   _____
21. &   _____
22. Inc.   _____
23. 2 yrs. _____
24. 4 ft.   _____

25. 96th St. _____
26. Ave.   _____
27. Blvd.   _____
28. Rd.   _____
29. Bldg.   _____
30. Feb.   _____
31. Aug.   _____
32. Dec.   _____
33. sq. ft.   _____
34. 1st   _____
35. 3rd   _____
36. 7th   _____
37. Thurs.   _____
38. Wed.   _____
39. NY   _____
40. CA   _____
41. USA   _____
42. UK   _____
43. @   _____
44. 1 cm   _____
45. $5   _____
46. 8 km   _____
47. CD   _____
48. PO Box   _____

The present perfect continuous tense is formed with *have/has been* and the present participle of the main verb.

> I have been working. We have been working.
>
> You have been working. You have been working.
>
> He has been working. They have been working.
>
> She has been working.
>
> It has been working.

The present perfect continuous tense is used to describe an action that began in the past and is continuing in the present.

> We *have been living* here for eight years.
>
> Bruce *has been studying* law since last year.

Write the present perfect continuous tense of the verb in parentheses.

1. She (study) English for two years.   *has been studying*

2. We (live) in this house since last March.   _____

3. I (try) to reach you by phone for the last hour.   _____

4. He (drive) that same old car for at least ten years.   _____

5. She (feel) much better recently.   _____

6. He (sit) on that bench for several hours.   _____

7. Rose (work) on that same problem for several days.   _____

8. They (talk) on the telephone for over an hour.   _____

9. She naturally speaks English well because she (speak)
    it all her life.   _____

10. He (work) in that same office ever since I first met him.   _____

11. They (listen) to music all evening.   _____

12. I (wait) here for you for almost an hour.   _____

13. It (rain) all day long.   _____

14. You (whistle) that same tune for the last hour.   _____

15. She (study) music since she was a child.   _____

16. She (wear) that same hat for more than a year.   _____

17. They (work) there for a long time.   _____

18. We (plan) this trip for many months.   _____

Negative Form

Form the negative of the present perfect continuous tense by placing *not* after *have* or *has*. The contracted forms are generally used.

She has been studying English for a long time.	She *hasn't* been studying English for a long time.
They have been working a lot this week.	They *haven't* been working a lot this week.

Change the sentence to the negative form. Use contractions.

1. Clara has been teaching here for a long time. *hasn't been teaching*

2. Bob has been feeling well lately. _____

3. They have been discussing the problem all morning. _____

4. The dog has been following the boy everywhere. _____

5. John and Mary have been dating each other. _____

6. Martha has been speaking English all her life. _____

7. My cousins have been staying at our house all summer. _____

8. It has been snowing all afternoon. _____

9. Gina has been studying music since she was a child. _____

10. We have been planning this trip for a long time. _____

11. The children have been sitting there all morning. _____

12. Mr. Park has been working here all his life. _____

13. Rosa has been teaching French since she graduated from college. _____

14. We have been waiting for him all evening. _____

15. They have been listening the whole time. _____

Question Form

To form questions in the present perfect continuous tense, place *have* or *has* before the subject. To form questions with question words, such as *How long*, *Where*, or *Why*, place the question word before *have* or *has*.

She has been studying English for a long time.	*Has she* been studying English for a long time?
	How long has she been studying English?

Write questions using the question words in parentheses. Use pronouns and change I *and* we *to* you.

1. She has been teaching here for a long time. (How long)

   How long has she been teaching here?

2. He has been feeling sick lately. (How long)

   _____

3. They have been discussing the problem for a while. (How long)

   _____

4. The dog has been following the boy everywhere. (Why)

   _____

5. We have been living in a new house since last summer. (Where)

   _____

6. She has been reading something all week. (What)

   _____

7. They have been staying at the beach. (How long)

   _____

8. It has been snowing for a long time. (How long)

   _____

9. I have been thinking about something all morning. (What)

   _____

10. We have been planning this trip for a long time. (How long)

    _____

11. The children have been sitting there all morning. (Why)

    _____

12. Ms. Wilson has been working here for a while. (How long)

    _____

SINCE, FOR, AGO

Since tells when the action began.

> **They have lived here *since* 1978.**

For shows the length of time of the action in the present, past, and future tenses.

> **We have lived here *for* six years.   She'll stay in Europe *for* a year.**

Ago refers to how much time back in the past something happened.

> **My ancestors arrived in this country 175 years *ago*.**

Write since, for, *or* ago *in the blank.*

1. I met him on the street about two weeks _____.   _____*ago*_____

2. He has been studying English _____ last January.   _____

3. She has been studying English _____ two years.   _____

4. I visited them in Santiago about six months _____.   _____

5. He stayed with us _____ about six months.   _____

6. Clara has lived in that same house _____ many years.   _____

7. They have lived there _____ 1998.   _____

8. She has never been the same _____ he went away.   _____

9. He has been sick _____ several days.   _____

10. She has been sick _____ Wednesday.   _____

11. How long _____ did the accident happen?   _____

12. I haven't seen Chris _____ last Christmas.   _____

13. We talked _____ about two hours.   _____

14. She has been in the hospital _____ July.   _____

15. He left for Tokyo three days _____.   _____

16. I haven't talked with her _____ yesterday.   _____

17. I talked with her _____ a few minutes yesterday.   _____

18. Mr. Pelli has been teaching English ever _____ he returned
    to the United States.   _____

19. She first began to teach English about three years _____.   _____

42

To form the past perfect tense, use *had* and the past participle of the main verb.

I had finished.	We had finished.
You had finished.	You had finished.
He had finished.	They had finished.
She had finished.	
It had finished.	

The past perfect tense is used to tell about an action that began and ended in the past before another past action. It is used with the past tense, either stated or implied.

> By the time you arrived, they *had* already *left*.
>
> It *had burned* down before the first fire trucks arrived.

Write the past perfect tense of the verb in parentheses.

1. He told me that he (visit) Miami several times before. — *had visited*

2. I thought it was the stranger who (steal) the money. — _____

3. I saw that we (take) the wrong road. — _____

4. She (have) her lunch already when we got there. — _____

5. By the time we were ready to leave, he (find) his keys. — _____

6. I didn't want to go with them because I (see) the movie already. — _____

7. When we arrived, they already (leave). — _____

8. I visited many of the places where I (play) as a boy. — _____

9. We got there just ten minutes after he (leave). — _____

10. She (live) there two years when the war began. — _____

11. After he (look) everywhere for his wallet, he decided to borrow some money. — _____

12. By the time I spoke to her, she already (take) the money to the bank. — _____

13. I was sure that he (have) the same trouble before. — _____

14. The police said that they (receive) several similar reports the same evening. — _____

15. What did he say he (do) with the money? — _____

PAST PERFECT TENSE

Negative Form

Form the negative of the past perfect tense by placing *not* after *had*. The contracted form is generally used.

She had studied English for a long time.	She *hadn't studied* English for a long time.

Write the negative past perfect form of the verb in parentheses. Use the contracted form.

1. When I got your message, I (receive) the package yet.   *hadn't received*

2. Bob (study) English before he came to this school.   _____

3. When Phil applied for the job, he (have) a lot of work experience.   _____

4. They (eat) dinner yet when they got home.   _____

5. We (buy) our tickets yet when we got on the train.   _____

6. Martha and Jim (meet) each other before they started working here.   _____

7. I (finish) all the exercises in the book when the semester ended.   _____

8. I told them that I (see) that movie yet.   _____

9. I thought she (leave) the office early.   _____

10. We (live) there long when they built the new road.   _____

11. When Tom called, Susan (arrive) home yet.   _____

12. When Sarah got to class, she (do) her homework.   _____

13. I (work) here for very long when my boss quit.   _____

14. When we arrived, they (finish) eating dinner yet.   _____

15. The pilots (arrive) when we boarded the plane.   _____

16. The children (wash) the dishes yet.   _____

17. The leaves (fall) yet when the first snow came.   _____

18. The orchestra (begin) to play when the electricity failed.   _____

Question Form

To form questions in the past perfect tense, place *had* before the subject. To form questions with questions words such as, *How long, Where,* or *How many,* place the question word before *had*.

She had studied English for a long time.   *Had she* studied English for a long time?
How long had she studied English?

Make questions using the subject and verb in parentheses.

1. Where (Robert, study) before he came to this school? <u> had Robert studied </u>

2. How long (Lily and Joe, know) each other before they got married? <u>   </u>

3. How many languages (Lee, study) before he studied English? <u>   </u>

4. How long (you, live) in that house when you finally decided to sell it? <u>   </u>

5. Where (he, work) before he got this job? <u>   </u>

6. How many books (Sylvia, write) before she finally got one published? <u>   </u>

7. How many hours (you, work) when you decided to take a rest? <u>   </u>

8. How long (Otto, work) there when he retired? <u>   </u>

9. How many miles (you, walk) when you stopped for lunch? <u>   </u>

10. How many times (Isabel, enter) the contest before she finally won? <u>   </u>

11. How long (Michael, study) before he got his degree? <u>   </u>

12. How many times (you, see) that movie before you saw it with me. <u>   </u>

13. How long (we, wait) for them by the time they arrived? <u>   </u>

14. Where (Ms. Kim, teach) before she taught here? <u>   </u>

15. How many children (she, have) before the twins were born? <u>   </u>

16. Where (they, hold) their meetings before they got this office? <u>   </u>

NEGATIVE FORM

Review 5

Change the sentence to the negative form. Use contractions.

1. He knows English well.   *doesn't know*

2. She left yesterday for California. _____

3. Anne is a very good student. _____

4. I wanted to take a walk. _____

5. He has studied English for many years. _____

6. He told her all about his plans. _____

7. They will return on Wednesday. _____

8. He is having his lunch now. _____

9. They have left for the station. _____

10. She can speak French well. _____

11. You must tell him about it. _____

12. They are going to the movies with us. _____

13. It is a beautiful day. _____

14. It was a very pleasant day. _____

15. She has worked in that office for many years. _____

16. They have been living there for a long time. _____

17. She has to work tonight. _____

18. She had to go to the hospital to see a friend. _____

19. He came to the lesson yesterday. _____

20. They are making good progress in their studies. _____

21. He told me to wait for him. _____

22. She prepares her lessons carefully. _____

23. They were playing tennis at the time. _____

24. Julia has finished that work. _____

25. Suki is planting flowers in the garden. _____

26. We had our work finished by three o'clock. _____

27. I had had two cups of coffee already when they arrived. _____

Change the sentence to the question form.

1. She works on the tenth floor.   *Does she work*
2. He gave her the message.   _____
3. She is a good friend of hers.   _____
4. We are going to the movies tonight.   _____
5. They will return home on Wednesday.   _____
6. He left his keys at home.   _____
7. Marcia can swim very well.   _____
8. She is going to study Chinese next year.   _____
9. He has read that novel before.   _____
10. She has been studying English for many years.   _____
11. She is very eager to learn English well.   _____
12. We have to have more practice in conversation.   _____
13. Robert had to leave for New York yesterday.   _____
14. He will return in a few days.   _____
15. They were having lunch at the time.   _____
16. They built that bridge last year.   _____
17. They will deliver the merchandise tomorrow.   _____
18. She was here at three o'clock.   _____
19. It is almost three o'clock.   _____
20. The wind is blowing very hard.   _____
21. There were many people in the park.   _____
22. The child cut herself badly.   _____
23. The boy ran between the two cars.   _____
24. The doorbell is ringing now.   _____

PREPOSITIONS 3

Write the correct preposition or particle in the blank.

1. The exercise was too difficult _____ him to do.   ____*for*____
2. It was kind _____ you to do that for her.   _____
3. She is worried _____ her husband's health.   _____
4. They are putting _____ several new buildings on that block.   _____
5. The bus doesn't stop _____ this corner.   _____
6. Have you heard _____ Sally's new baby?   _____
7. Nora wants to go _____ a diet.   _____
8. What are they laughing _____?   _____
9. What was he talking _____?   _____
10. He has been studying English _____ three years.   _____
11. We usually take our vacation _____ July.   _____
12. We hung the pictures _____ the fireplace.   _____
13. The temperature dropped from ten degrees above zero to ten degrees _____ zero.   _____
14. Why don't you sit _____ a more comfortable chair?   _____
15. That building seems to be _____ fire.   _____
16. The elevator is not running today. It is _____ of order.   _____
17. What is the matter _____ him?   _____
18. I make many mistakes _____ spelling.   _____
19. I see Josie in the cafeteria _____ time to time.   _____
20. I will get _____ touch with you next week.   _____
21. He seems to be _____ a hurry.   _____
22. She was absent _____ class twice last week.   _____
23. I left my coat _____ the bus.   _____
24. This book belongs _____ Nancy.   _____

Select the correct form. Write your answer in the blank.

1. Marie has worked in that office (for, since) many years.   _____for_____

2. By the time we got there, Tony (had, has) left.   _____

3. When we arrived, Alice (read, was reading) the newspaper.   _____

4. This book is mine, and that one is (your, yours).   _____

5. We (must, had to) go to the hospital last night to see a friend
   who is sick.   _____

6. We (haven't to, don't have to) work tomorrow because it is a
   holiday.   _____

7. We (have been, were) in California for two months last winter.   _____

8. When Marc got home, Marie (cooks, was cooking) dinner.   _____

9. I (bought, was buying) some new CDs yesterday.   _____

10. What time did you (leave, left) home this morning?   _____

11. Hurry! The bus (comes, is coming).   _____

12. They (have, are having) their dinner now.   _____

13. The teacher explained (us, to us) the meaning of the word.   _____

14. Rita wants (me to go, that I go) to the movies with her.   _____

15. He gave (me, to me) all the money he had.   _____

16. The wind (is blowing, blows) very hard during the month of March.   _____

17. I didn't hear (someone, anyone) in the next room.   _____

18. We (went, have gone) to the movies last night.   _____

19. We (are, have been) friends for many years.   _____

20. Julio (said, told) that he could not come to the party.   _____

21. Listen! The birds (sing, are singing).   _____

22. He is (a, an) old friend of hers.   _____

23. We (didn't have, hadn't had) anything to eat all day, so we
    ordered a lot of food.   _____

CONTRACTIONS

Review

To be

I'm	we're
you're	you're
he's	they're
she's	
it's	

Certain auxiliaries are also commonly used in the contracted form.

> I'll (I will), I've (I have), you've (you have), she'd (she had), etc.

Remember that we usually use the contracted form with negatives and auxiliary verbs.

> isn't, wasn't, won't, can't, don't, didn't, haven't, etc.

Change the words in italics to the contracted form.

1. *I am* very busy today.   *I'm*
2. *You are* a good friend of his.   _____
3. *She is* going to the movies with us.   _____
4. *It is* raining.   _____
5. *She is* the best student in the class.   _____
6. *We are* very old friends.   _____
7. *They are* having their lunch now.   _____
8. *There is* someone in the next room.   _____
9. *You are* here too early.   _____
10. *I will* meet you at six o'clock.   _____
11. *You will* be late if you don't hurry.   _____
12. *She will* return next week.   _____
13. *We will* be back at five o'clock.   _____
14. I *do not* know her well.   _____
15. He *does not* speak English.   _____
16. They *did not* come to the meeting last night.   _____
17. I *will not* be able to meet you tomorrow.   _____
18. They *are not* going to the movies with us.   _____
19. I *have not* seen that movie.   _____

Use *in order to* or *to* followed by the simple form of the verb to express purpose. The short form (*to*) is more common in everyday conversation.

> We went to the hospital *in order to* see our friend.
>
> We went to the hospital *to* see our friend.

For is used before nouns to express purpose.

> I went to the store *for* some ice cream.
>
> She's shopping *for* a new stereo.

Write to *or* for *in the blank.*

1. She went to town _____ buy some gas.   _____to_____

2. She has gone to the store _____ some computer paper.   _____

3. He went to the bank _____ some money.   _____

4. He went to the bank _____ get some money.   _____

5. He is going to go to Florida _____ his health.   _____

6. Barbara came _____ the CDs that you promised to lend her.   _____

7. I have to go to the post office _____ mail a package.   _____

8. He first came to this country _____ visit his relatives.   _____

9. I'll stop at the theater _____ the tickets that you bought.   _____

10. I'll stop at the theater _____ pick up the tickets that you bought.   _____

11. We are going to the airport _____ meet some friends.   _____

12. Martha is coming to our house tonight _____ dinner.   _____

13. He is coming to the United States just _____ study English.   _____

14. Some friends came _____ visit us last night.   _____

15. He often waits after class just _____ talk with the teacher.   _____

16. She went to the florist's _____ buy some flowers.   _____

17. Felicia went _____ see her dentist about her toothache.   _____

18. My parents had to hire someone _____ fix the roof.   _____

INDIRECT OBJECT POSITION

Review

If the indirect object follows the direct object, we use the preposition *to* or *for*. If the indirect object precedes the direct object, we do not use a preposition.

He handed the phone *to me*.	He handed *me* the phone.
I bought a new tennis racquet *for Ruth*.	I bought *Ruth* a new tennis racquet.

Some verbs that function this way are *give*, *send*, *bring*, *tell*, *write*, and *buy*.

Change the sentence so that the indirect object comes before the direct object. Write the main verb and the indirect object in the blank.

1. He gave the money to her.   *gave her*

2. I gave the tickets to Antonia. _____

3. I sent some money to him for his birthday. _____

4. Don't show these things to Rudy. _____

5. She paid the money to the landlord. _____

6. He sold the books to his friend. _____

7. I took the flowers to her. _____

8. She brought a box of candy to me. _____

9. He bought a new car for his wife. _____

10. She brought many presents to us from abroad. _____

11. I will send an e-mail message to them tomorrow. _____

12. She gave the money to her father to put in the bank. _____

13. We sent some flowers to Ms. Pappas. _____

14. I told the whole story to Sharon. _____

15. He gave a piece of the candy to each of us. _____

16. He lent a large sum of money to his brother. _____

17. Please hand those plates to me. _____

18. She sent a postcard to each of them. _____

19. They will send the merchandise to us next week. _____

20. He lent his car to us for the afternoon. _____

21. She may bring a present for me from Bali. _____

Review

Study and memorize this list of irregular verbs. Many of these verbs end in an *n* sound in the past participle form.

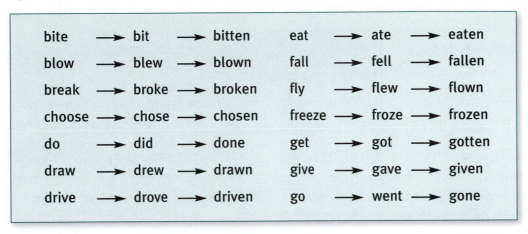

bite	→ bit	→ bitten	eat	→ ate	→ eaten
blow	→ blew	→ blown	fall	→ fell	→ fallen
break	→ broke	→ broken	fly	→ flew	→ flown
choose	→ chose	→ chosen	freeze	→ froze	→ frozen
do	→ did	→ done	get	→ got	→ gotten
draw	→ drew	→ drawn	give	→ gave	→ given
drive	→ drove	→ driven	go	→ went	→ gone

Write the correct form of the verb in parentheses.

1. Yesterday the wind (blow) down the tree in front of our house. _____blew_____

2. All the birds have (fly) south for the winter. _____

3. He told us that he had (drive) the car more than a hundred thousand miles. _____

4. Last night thieves (break) into our neighbor's home. _____

5. It is the third time that someone has (break) into her home. _____

6. While he was skating in the park yesterday, Alex (fall) and hurt himself. _____

7. He has (fall) many times before but never hurt himself. _____

8. We (do) some exercises similar to these last week. _____

9. I went to the bank this morning and (draw) out all my money. _____

10. We (eat) lunch in the school cafeteria yesterday. _____

11. It was so cold last winter in Europe that more than a hundred people (freeze) to death. _____

12. I met Tom yesterday and (give) him the money that I owed him. _____

13. At the meeting last night, we (choose) Nina as the new president of our club. _____

14. That dog has (bite) several people. _____

15. Have you (do) your homework yet? _____

In addition to *will* + the simple form of the verb to express the future tense, we form the future tense with the appropriate form of *to be going to* and the simple form of the verb. The contracted forms are normally used.

I *am going to* fly.	(*I'm going to* fly.)	We *are going to* fly.	(*We're going to* fly.)
You *are going to* fly.	(*You're going to* fly.)		
He *is going to* fly.	(*He's going to* fly.)	You *are going to* fly.	(*You're going to* fly.)
She *is going to* fly.	(*She's going to* fly.)		
It *is going to* fly.	(*It's going to* fly.)	They *are going to* fly.	(*They're going to* fly.)

We generally shorten such sentences as "He *is going to go* to Mexico on his vacation" to "He *is going* to Mexico on his vacation."

Write the correct form of the verb in parentheses.

1. He (wait) for us after the lesson.   *is going to wait*
2. Michel (teach) me how to swim.
3. Hurry! We (be) late for the lesson.
4. She (meet) us after the theater.
5. We (stay) home and watch TV tonight.
6. He (go) to Mexico on his vacation.
7. She (take) an engineering class this summer.
8. We (go) to the beach this afternoon.
9. The paper says that it (rain) tomorrow.
10. We (eat) out tonight.
11. Martin (have) dinner with us.
12. After dinner we (go) to the theater.
13. She (get) married in June.
14. They (spend) their honeymoon in Bermuda.
15. Juanita (ask) Tom for a date.
16. You (be) late for class if you don't hurry.
17. We (go) to the movies tonight.
18. They (fly) to Rangoon.

In Past Tense

The past form of *going to* indicates an action that was planned but did not happen. To form the past tense, use the correct past tense form of *to be going to* and the simple form of the verb.

I was going to move.	We were going to move.
You were going to move.	You were going to move.
He was going to move.	They were going to move.
She was going to move.	
It was going to move.	

We generally shorten such sentences as "I *was going to go* shopping this afternoon" to "I *was going* shopping this afternoon."

Write the correct form of the past tense of to be going to *and the simple form of the verb. Use the long form of* to be going to go.

1. We (watch) TV last night, but the electricity went out.   *were going to watch*

2. I (go) shopping this afternoon, but I had too much work to do at home.

3. She (study) abroad last year but decided to stay on campus.

4. We (go) to the beach yesterday, but it rained too hard.

5. He (see) a doctor about the pain in his back, but suddenly the pain disappeared.

6. We (buy) a new computer but decided to wait until next year.

7. They (visit) us last night but later changed their plans.

8. He always said that he (be) a doctor when he grew up, but he finally went into business.

9. We (eat) out last night, but the weather was too bad.

10. I (send) him an e-mail message but decided to call instead.

11. She (lend) me the money, but her husband was opposed to it.

When the main verb of the sentence is in the past tense, all dependent verbs are generally in the past tense, too.

> **Jerry *says* he *will* come to the party.**   **Jerry *said* he *would* come to the party.**
>
> **I *know* this test *will* be difficult.**   **I *knew* this test *would* be difficult.**

Note the irregular past tense form of the following auxiliary verbs:

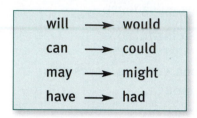

will	→ would
can	→ could
may	→ might
have	→ had

Select the correct form of the verb in parentheses. Write your answer in the blank.

1. Sarah said that she (will, would) be late for the lesson. _____would_____

2. I thought it (is, was) going to rain. _____

3. He didn't think he (can, could) go with us. _____

4. The newspaper said that the weather today (will, would) be cold. _____

5. He said that his first name (is, was) Robert. _____

6. I asked him where he (lives, lived). _____

7. She said her name (is, was) Brigitte. _____

8. I asked him whether he (likes, liked) New Delhi. _____

9. The man told me that he (lives, lived) in Mexico. _____

10. He also said that he (can, could) speak Spanish well. _____

11. I thought I (will, would) be late for class. _____

12. She said she (may, might) go with us to the movies tonight. _____

13. I didn't know what his last name (is, was). _____

14. She told me she (has lost, had lost) her pocketbook. _____

15. She explained to me what the word (means, meant). _____

16. I asked the boy how old he (is, was). _____

17. He told me that he (will, would) help me with the work. _____

18. I thought I (may, might) be too late to see her. _____

19. I saw at once that he (is, was) a serious student. _____

The letter *s* is pronounced *s* in words such as *pass, this, see,* and *ask.* The letter *s* is pronounced *z* in words such as *his, does, rose,* and *goes.*

Write s *or* z *to show how the letter is pronounced in each word.*

1.	easy	__z__		23.	this	_____
2.	pass	__s__		24.	these	_____
3.	mouse	_____		25.	those	_____
4.	bus	_____		26.	kiss	_____
5.	news	_____		27.	his	_____
6.	raise	_____		28.	goes	_____
7.	seat	_____		29.	some	_____
8.	does	_____		30.	first	_____
9.	comes	_____		31.	cousin	_____
10.	eats	_____		32.	tries	_____
11.	rose	_____		33.	brings	_____
12.	class	_____		34.	likes	_____
13.	trays	_____		35.	puts	_____
14.	peas	_____		36.	dogs	_____
15.	tennis	_____		37.	cats	_____
16.	knows	_____		38.	was	_____
17.	nose	_____		39.	case	_____
18.	books	_____		40.	movies	_____
19.	eyes	_____		41.	plays	_____
20.	pens	_____		42.	cause	_____
21.	dress	_____		43.	cost	_____
22.	closed	_____		44.	is	_____

PRONUNCIATION OF *ED* IN VERBS

The final *ed* in the past tense of regular verbs takes two different pronunciations:

a. When *ed* is added to a verb ending in an unvoiced consonant (*p, t, f, k, s,* etc.), the final *d* is pronounced *t*.

b. When *ed* is added to a verb ending in a voiced consonant (*b, d, v, g, z, l,* etc.), or in a vowel sound, the final *d* is pronounced *d*.

Write t *or* d *to show how the* ed *is pronounced in each word.*

1.	lived	*d*	22.	boiled	
2.	picked	*t*	23.	finished	
3.	jumped		24.	burned	
4.	placed		25.	filled	
5.	hurried		26.	passed	
6.	rushed		27.	excused	
7.	joked		28.	mailed	
8.	killed		29.	slipped	
9.	looked		30.	liked	
10.	dropped		31.	used	
11.	turned		32.	changed	
12.	crossed		33.	worked	
13.	entered		34.	studied	
14.	stopped		35.	talked	
15.	earned		36.	spelled	
16.	knocked		37.	thanked	
17.	saved		38.	washed	
18.	played		39.	poured	
19.	wished		40.	walked	
20.	showed		41.	pulled	
21.	closed		42.	tried	

Expressions with *to get*

To get (someplace) means "to arrive."

> I *got* home late last night.   Her flight *gets* here at ten P.M.

To get means "to buy."

> He *got* a new suit on sale.   We're *getting* a new computer for the office.

To get, with various adjectives, means "to become."

> Gabriela *got angry* when you said that.   I always *get hungry* at this time of day.

To get is used in many phrasal verbs, for example, *to get up, to get on, to get in, to get over.*

Change the words in italics to a form of to get.

1. He *became angry* with us because we left so early.   ____got angry____

2. I didn't *arrive home* until almost eight o'clock.   _____

3. He *entered* the elevator as soon as the door opened.   _____

4. How long will it take you to *prepare* for the party?   _____

5. The plane *arrives* there about noon.   _____

6. She always *boards* the bus at this corner.   _____

7. She always *leaves* the bus at 79th Street.   _____

8. I *become very tired* if I have to walk too far.   _____

9. Amina *became excited* when she heard the good news.   _____

10. It took her several months to *recover from* the death of her friend.   _____

11. Sam *entered* the car first, and then I followed him.   _____

12. I usually *arrive at* my office at about nine o'clock.   _____

13. I seldom *reach home* before seven o'clock.   _____

14. Mr. Smith drank coffee so that he wouldn't *become sleepy* on the long drive.   _____

15. They plan to *marry* in June.   _____

SILENT LETTERS

Write the consonant that is written but not pronounced.

1. knife   _k_
2. answer   _w_
3. handsome   _____
4. Christmas   _____
5. island   _____
6. doubt   _____
7. knee   _____
8. wrestle   _____
9. honest   _____
10. often   _____
11. knew   _____
12. sign   _____
13. dumb   _____
14. match   _____
15. walk   _____
16. could   _____
17. talk   _____
18. knock   _____
19. know   _____
20. Wednesday   _____
21. pneumonia   _____
22. climb   _____
23. should   _____
24. aisle   _____
25. whole   _____

26. write   _____
27. fasten   _____
28. castle   _____
29. hymn   _____
30. scissors   _____
31. lamb   _____
32. gnaw   _____
33. limb   _____
34. wrong   _____
35. wrist   _____
36. listen   _____
37. sword   _____
38. comb   _____
39. knot   _____
40. kneel   _____
41. czar   _____
42. half   _____
43. ghost   _____
44. whistle   _____
45. scent   _____
46. calf   _____
47. ledge   _____
48. hour   _____
49. scene   _____
50. thumb   _____

Write the correct preposition or particle in the blank.

1. He is not interested _____ English.   _____in_____

2. We arrived _____ Boston at exactly six o'clock.   _____

3. She lives far _____ the station.   _____

4. We went to the beach in spite _____ the bad weather.   _____

5. Sue sits _____ front of me in chemistry class.   _____

6. The police officer ran _____ the thief but could not catch him.   _____

7. Mohammed is mad _____ me because I won't go to the beach
   with him.   _____

8. Ana is always trying to borrow money _____ someone.   _____

9. I'll be back _____ an hour.   _____

10. It is dark in this room. Please turn _____ the light.   _____

11. The wind blew my hat _____.   _____

12. The dog tried to jump _____ the fence, but the fence was too
    high for him.   _____

13. The man died _____ pneumonia.   _____

14. They called off the game because _____ rain.   _____

15. Her English is improving little _____ little.   _____

16. The teacher crossed _____ several words in my composition.   _____

17. The vending machine is not working today. It must be
    out _____ order.   _____

18. Ming did not do very well _____ his last exam.   _____

19. Maureen is very enthusiastic _____ her new job.   _____

20. He left his hat _____ the chair.   _____

21. He likes to walk _____ the rain.   _____

22. Rosemary plays the piano _____ ear.   _____

23. We plan to go to Lima _____ plane.   _____

24. She is the girl I spoke to you _____.   _____

Select the correct form. Write your answer in the blank.

1. They (was, were) both sitting in the park when I saw them.   *were*

2. When I met him, he already (has had, had had) his lunch.

3. Ali (saved, has saved) five hundred dollars since January.

4. Last night, while we (walked, were walking) home, we met some old friends.

5. Nina (went, has gone) to the dance with Sal last night.

6. We have (eaten, ate) at this restaurant several times.

7. He gave (to me, me) some money.

8. She asked (me to wait, that I wait) for her.

9. He (said, told) that he would be back at six o'clock.

10. She said her last name (is, was) Castro.

11. He said that he (will, would) wait for us after class.

12. Ruth sat (between, among) Sachiko and Stephanie.

13. Liz always (sits, is sitting) at this desk.

14. Look! It (begins, is beginning) to snow.

15. I (am, was) going to go swimming yesterday, but it was too cold.

16. He called up Gina (to, for) invite her to dinner.

17. She spends (a lot of, many) time on her English.

18. He has always been a good friend of (her, hers).

19. Yesterday I met an old classmate of (me, my, mine).

20. He (said, told) us that he would meet us at noon.

21. Chris was sick yesterday and (can, could) not come to class.

22. When I got there, they (were having, had) dinner.

23. Gia (closed, was closing) the windows before she left the house.

24. We already (make, made) an appointment for next week.

25. She (had to have, must have) her paper finished yesterday.

26. I was surprised to see him because he (hasn't, hadn't) told me he (is, was) coming.

In the passive voice, the subject receives the action of the verb. Form the passive voice by using the appropriate form of *to be* and the past participle of the main verb.

Active Voice	*Passive Voice*
She repairs my shoes.	My shoes *are repaired* by her.
He cleans the house.	The house *is cleaned* by him.
He will repair my shoes.	My shoes *will be repaired* by him.
He has repaired my shoes.	My shoes *have been repaired* by him.

Change the sentence from the active to the passive voice. Write complete sentences. Put all adverbial expressions at the end of the sentence.

1. Mr. Dodd teaches this class.   *This class is taught by Mr. Dodd.*
2. She writes many newspaper articles. _____
3. The maid cleans the room every day. _____
4. Everyone hears their quarrels. _____
5. The letter carrier delivers the mail. _____
6. The secretary writes all the letters. _____
7. Everyone enjoys her speeches. _____
8. They sell the magazine everywhere. _____
9. She corrects our exercises at home. _____
10. Joe prepares dinner every night. _____
11. They deliver the mail at ten o'clock. _____
12. A messenger brings urgent information. _____
13. They sign the documents in the courthouse. _____
14. She brings presents from Hong Kong. _____
15. The teacher corrects our compositions. _____
16. They print the books in Boston. _____
17. He cuts the grass once a week. _____
18. They send the papers by express mail. _____
19. The lawyer prepares the contracts. _____

Form the passive voice in different verb tenses by using the appropriate form of the verb *to be*.

Active Voice	Passive Voice
He cleaned the house.	The house *was cleaned* by him.
They will paint our house.	Our house *will be painted* by them.
That company has opened several new stores.	Several new stores *have been opened* by that company.
Akira had already seen the movie.	The movie *had already been seen* by Akira.

Change the sentence from the active to the passive voice. Write complete sentences. Put all adverbial expressions at the end of the sentence.

1. Mr. Sato taught the class.   *The class was taught by Mr. Sato.*

2. Someone took the money.   _____

3. The letter carrier had delivered the mail.   _____

4. He has signed the letters.   _____

5. She has written many books.   _____

6. Marianne paid the bills by check.   _____

7. They will finish the work tomorrow.   _____

8. He had finished the work in time.   _____

9. They have planned the party.   _____

10. Native Americans grew corn in Mexico.   _____

11. He has designed several buildings.   _____

12. He had signed the contract previously.   _____

13. She broke the plate in anger.   _____

14. Julia saw the accident on her way home.   _____

15. They had bought the tickets.   _____

16. They have found the child at last.   _____

17. Sonia will plant the trees.   _____

18. They prepared the dinner.   _____

19. She will send it immediately.   _____

20. He used the key to open the door.   _____

Form the passive voice of *can*, *have to*, *may*, *must*, *ought to*, and *should* with *be* and the past participle of the main verb.

I *must* finish this work quickly.	This work *must be finished* (by me) quickly.
You *can* protect the plants with plastic bags.	The plants *can be protected* (by you) with plastic bags.
She *should* do her work on the computer.	Her work *should be done* (by her) on the computer.

Form the passive voice with infinitives by using *be* and the past participle of the main verb.

He has *to do* it today.	It has *to be done* (by him) today.
They are going *to take* it.	It is going *to be taken* by them.

Form the passive in the continuous tenses with *being* and the past participle of the main verb.

Someone *is watering* the flowers.	The flowers *are being watered*.

If it is not important to state the doer of the action, the *by* phrase can be omitted.

Change the sentence from the active to the passive voice. Write complete sentences. Leave out the by *phrase if the subject is a pronoun. Put all adverbial expressions at the end of the sentence.*

1. We can finish this today.   *This can be finished today.*

2. The museum may keep it for two weeks. _____

3. You can pay the bill later. _____

4. We have to deliver it tomorrow. _____

5. They can't put those things there. _____

6. They must send it at once. _____

7. They should deliver it today. _____

8. You ought to write it now. _____

9. All the students must complete this work. _____

10. They may bring it later. _____

11. Linda can use this room. _____

12. She has to do it soon. _____

PASSIVE VOICE

Negative Form

Form negatives in the passive voice by placing *not* after the the correct form of the verb *to be*. When an auxiliary—such as *will*, *have*, or *can*—is used, *not* always follows the auxiliary. We generally use the contracted forms.

> The book *was not written (wasn't written)* by Ian Fleming.
>
> The film *will not be shown (won't be shown)* until next week.

Change the sentence to the negative form. Write the complete verb in the blank.

1. The book was published in France.   *was not published*

2. The books will be delivered on Wednesday. _____

3. These letters must be signed by the manager. _____

4. The thief was shot by a police officer. _____

5. This class is taught by Ellen Marks. _____

6. The package was wrapped very neatly. _____

7. The house was struck by lightning. _____

8. The mail has been delivered. _____

9. The war was followed by a serious economic depression. _____

10. The screams were heard by everyone. _____

11. This room can be used for our lesson. _____

12. The book was printed in Mexico. _____

13. The letters were sent by regular mail. _____

14. The merchandise will be delivered tomorrow. _____

15. The bill can be sent after the first of the month. _____

16. The money was taken by a visitor. _____

17. We were disappointed by the music. _____

18. The report will be written by Joe Trumbull. _____

19. The house had been decorated by a New York firm. _____

Question Form

Form questions in the passive voice by placing the correct form of the verb *to be* or an auxiliary verb before the subject.

> *Will that film* be shown on TV this year?
>
> *Was the best actor award* won by Tom Cruise?
>
> *Has your book* been published yet?

Change the sentence to the question form. Write the subject and the complete verb in the blank.

1. The man was shot by a police officer.   *Was the man shot*

2. The thief was captured by the police.   _____

3. The lecture will be attended by many important people.   _____

4. The dinner has been served by the host.   _____

5. We are invited to David's party.   _____

6. The work will be done by a Santa Fe firm.   _____

7. The city was destroyed by fire.   _____

8. These letters must be signed at once.   _____

9. America was discovered in 1492.   _____

10. The house has been struck by lightning.   _____

11. His book will be published next month.   _____

12. This project should be finished today.   _____

13. The mail is delivered at exactly nine o'clock.   _____

14. The poems are written by Connie.   _____

15. The car was destroyed in the accident.   _____

16. Their engagement will be announced soon.   _____

17. They will be married in New York.   _____

18. The meeting was held in Paris.   _____

19. It was attended by all the foreign ministers.   _____

20. All these books can be borrowed from the library.   _____

ARTICLES

Review

Write the definite or indefinite article in the blank. If no article is necessary, leave blank.

1. They say that _____ climate of Mexico is very pleasant.   _____the_____

2. I bought my new suit in _____ London.   _____

3. I have such _____ headache that I can hardly see.   _____

4. How do you like that kind of _____ weather?   _____

5. I enjoy walking along _____ Ocean Avenue.   _____

6. _____ Bank Street pier is popular on weekends.   _____

7. May I have a glass of _____ cold water?   _____

8. _____ water in this glass is not cold.   _____

9. This is one of _____ longest rivers in the world.   _____

10. Susan is _____ engineer.   _____

11. I will meet you in front of _____ Grand Central Station.   _____

12. _____ United States sent three astronauts to the moon in 1969.   _____

13. Have you ever visited _____ Australia?   _____

14. _____ English fought bravely in World War II.   _____

15. _____ English language is not difficult to learn.   _____

16. _____ day was so hot that we had to stop work.   _____

17. It was such _____ hot day that we had to stop work.   _____

18. We walked along Fifth Avenue as far as _____ Central Park.   _____

19. In general, it takes several years to learn _____ foreign language.   _____

20. He is _____ pharmacist.   _____

21. This is _____ Dominique's book.   _____

22. _____ Dominican Republic lies east of Cuba.   _____

23. We took a trip around _____ Mediterranean.   _____

24. _____ President Grey had a serious heart attack.   _____

25. _____ president will speak on TV tonight.   _____

Study and memorize this list of irregular verbs. Note that they terminate in an *n* sound in the past participle form.

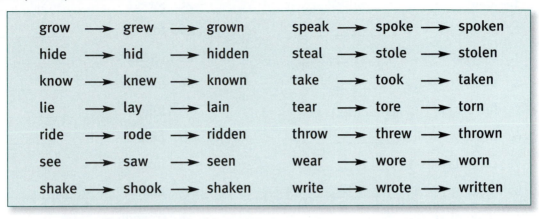

grow → grew → grown   speak → spoke → spoken

hide → hid → hidden   steal → stole → stolen

know → knew → known   take → took → taken

lie → lay → lain   tear → tore → torn

ride → rode → ridden   throw → threw → thrown

see → saw → seen   wear → wore → worn

shake → shook → shaken   write → wrote → written

Write the correct form of the verb in parentheses.

1. Someone broke into our house last night and (steal) our new TV.   *stole*

2. Look! You have (tear) your coat. _____

3. The dog has always (lie) in that position. _____

4. I have (know) Franco for many years. _____

5. After Solomon introduced us, we (shake) hands. _____

6. Michel (speak) to me about that matter yesterday. _____

7. The child has (grow) more than 6 inches in the last year. _____

8. Pedro got angry and (throw) the book on the table. _____

9. The child ran and (hide) behind a tree. _____

10. She has (wear) that hat every day for months. _____

11. Last night I stayed at home and (write) several letters. _____

12. Carlos (take) Monique to the dance last night. _____

13. I haven't (ride) in Sachiko's new car yet. _____

14. He was born in Mexico but (grow) up in California. _____

15. I haven't (see) Nina in several weeks. _____

16. Clara (tear) up the letter and then threw it away. _____

17. Grace and Jane have not (speak) to each other for several months. _____

18. Paul (know) Spain well because he had been there many times before. _____

19. I believe he has (know) about it for a long time. _____

Opposites 2

Write the opposite of the word.

1.	loser	*winner*	26.	sweet	_____
2.	strong	_____	27.	tall	_____
3.	everyone	_____	28.	useless	_____
4.	alive	_____	29.	increase	_____
5.	false	_____	30.	follow	_____
6.	polite	_____	31.	parent	_____
7.	careful	_____	32.	front	_____
8.	stop	_____	33.	raise	_____
9.	remember	_____	34.	tragedy	_____
10.	wrong	_____	35.	same	_____
11.	early	_____	36.	east	_____
12.	never	_____	37.	rise	_____
13.	slow	_____	38.	depart	_____
14.	effect	_____	39.	lost	_____
15.	smooth	_____	40.	tame	_____
16.	loosen	_____	41.	presence	_____
17.	wholesale	_____	42.	temporary	_____
18.	brave	_____	43.	victory	_____
19.	sell	_____	44.	private	_____
20.	quiet	_____	45.	enemy	_____
21.	dry	_____	46.	lend	_____
22.	tight	_____	47.	subtract	_____
23.	forward	_____	48.	guilty	_____
24.	complicated	_____	49.	common	_____
25.	empty	_____	50.	winter	_____

Comparative Form

The comparative form of one-syllable adjectives and adverbs adds *er*.

> cold ⟶ colder   fast ⟶ faster

The comparative form of adjectives and adverbs of more than one syllable usually uses *more*. However, two-syllable adjectives that end in *y* or *ow* add *er*. The *y* is changed to *i* before the *er* is added.

> expensive ⟶ more expensive   rapidly ⟶ more rapidly
>
> needy ⟶ needier   shallow ⟶ shallower

Remember the irregular forms of the following adjectives and adverbs:

> good ⟶ better   well ⟶ better
>
> bad ⟶ worse   badly ⟶ worse

Write the comparative form of the adjectives and adverbs + than.

1. Tokyo is (big) Chicago.   *bigger than*
2. Carmen is (intelligent) her sister. _____
3. He arrived (early) we expected. _____
4. This book is (interesting) that one. _____
5. The Amazon River is much (wide) the Orinoco River. _____
6. This exercise is (easy) the last one. _____
7. She sings (beautifully) her sister. _____
8. She drives even (fast) her father. _____
9. He returned (soon) we expected. _____
10. Some people speak English (clearly) others. _____
11. He goes there (often) I. _____
12. Your pronunciation is (good) Clara's. _____
13. The weather today is (cold) it was yesterday. _____
14. She is (busy) she has ever been before. _____
15. Diego works (hard) the other students. _____
16. She prepares her lessons (carefully) they. _____
17. They go to the movies (often) we. _____
18. I got up this morning (early) usual. _____

AS ... AS

As ... as expresses equality. The phrase may be used with both adjectives and adverbs.

> Lisa is *as* tall *as* Doug.
>
> Martin can run *as* fast *as* you can.
>
> I left the office *as* soon *as* I could.

Supply the phrase as ... as. *Change the adjective to its corresponding adverb form where necessary.*

1. Tomiko is (tall) her brother.   *as tall as*

2. This book was (expensive) that one.   _____

3. Mario is not (old) I.   _____

4. She can speak English (good) the teacher.   _____

5. Amanda can't swim (fast) I.   _____

6. I will be there (soon) possible.   _____

7. I did (good) I could on the examination.   _____

8. The boy ran home (fast) his legs could carry him.   _____

9. Telephone me (soon) you get home.   _____

10. I don't think it is (cold) it was yesterday.   _____

11. He came to the office (quick) he could.   _____

12. She can do the work (easy) I.   _____

13. I am not (tired) I was yesterday.   _____

14. She doesn't work (hard) the other students.   _____

15. Your pronunciation is certainly (good) mine.   _____

16. We go to the movies (often) we can.   _____

17. Naturally, I cannot speak English (rapid) the teacher.   _____

18. I do my homework (careful) I can.   _____

19. She plays the piano (beautiful) anyone I have ever heard.   _____

20. He is almost (rich) the queen.   _____

21. She visits us (often) she can.   _____

Use *some* in affirmative sentences. Use *any* in negative sentences.

| We took *some* money with us. | We didn't have *any* money with us. |

Use *someone, somebody, something,* and *somewhere* in affirmative sentences. Use *anyone, anybody, anything,* and *anywhere* in negative sentences.

| I saw *someone* standing in the shadows. | The witness said she hadn't seen *anything.* |

Select the correct form. Write your answer in the blank.

1. He doesn't have (some, any) friends there. _____any_____

2. The police found him (somewhere, anywhere) in Central Park. _____

3. I didn't see (someone, anyone) in Ms. Stein's office. _____

4. I didn't have (some, any) time to prepare my homework last night. _____

5. Irene has (some, any) very pretty Persian carpets. _____

6. Don't tell (someone, anyone) about this. _____

7. Rita didn't say (something, anything) to me about it. _____

8. I gave the old man (some, any) money. _____

9. He met her (somewhere, anywhere) in Europe. _____

10. I didn't have (some, any) money with me at the time. _____

11. My aunt didn't send me (something, anything) for my birthday. _____

12. I hear (someone, anyone) in the next room. _____

13. Juan said that he hadn't seen (someone, anyone) in the room. _____

14. There are (some, any) people waiting to see you. _____

15. The police didn't let (someone, anyone) see the prisoner. _____

16. Mr. and Mrs. Garcia don't have (some, any) children. _____

17. I lost my purse (somewhere, anywhere) between here and 79th Street. _____

WORD STRESS

Study and memorize the pronunciation of each word. Write the number of syllables of each word in the first column. Write an ordinal number in the second column to tell which syllable of each word is stressed (accented).

		NUMBER OF SYLLABLES	STRESSED SYLLABLE
1.	tomorrow	3	2nd
2.	newspaper		
3.	cafeteria		
4.	communicate		
5.	continuous		
6.	admiration		
7.	discovery		
8.	president		
9.	dangerous		
10.	medicine		
11.	repeated		
12.	appeared		
13.	imagination		
14.	government		
15.	announced		
16.	disappointed		
17.	important		
18.	suggestion		
19.	returned		
20.	computer		
21.	unable		
22.	popularity		
23.	marriage		

Write the correct form of the verb in parentheses.

1. They (have) dinner when we arrived.   *were having*

2. I saw that, a few miles back, we (take) the wrong road. _____

3. Eric always (get up) at the same time every morning. _____

4. I (see) Helen at the airport yesterday. _____

5. But I (not see) her since then. _____

6. Sally, who is in the hospital, (be) there for about a month. _____

7. We (live) in São Paolo from 1995 to 2003. _____

8. I (work) on the computer when you called. _____

9. Listen! Someone (knock) at the door. _____

10. When we lived in San Diego, we often (take) trips by car to Mexico. _____

11. Please be more quiet. The baby (sleep). _____

12. The sun always (rise) in the east. _____

13. Up to now, I (not be) farther west than Chicago. _____

14. Lee said that he already (see) that movie. _____

15. I met a friend yesterday whom I (not see) in five years. _____

16. We (live) in France when the war broke out. _____

17. By the time they arrived, we (finish) our dinner. _____

18. Look! The tree (begin) to bloom. _____

19. Look! Antonia (cross) the street. _____

20. We (arrive) at school every morning at eight o'clock. _____

21. When the teacher arrived, the children (make) a lot of noise. _____

22. Ruth Davila (teach) in that school ever since she graduated from college. _____

23. Art says that he (come) back again tomorrow. _____

24. Gabriela said that she (come) back again tomorrow. _____

25. I (see) him after class tomorrow. _____

Write the correct preposition or particle in the blank.

1. Both Alice and Marianne were absent _____ school yesterday.   _____*from*_____

2. Lucia bought a ticket _____ Chicago at the station.   _____

3. I'll be over to see you _____ Wednesday night.   _____

4. I wrote a note to thank them _____ the nice gifts.   _____

5. What is the word _____ *eggs* in Spanish?   _____

6. He plans to take a trip _____ the world next year.   _____

7. A scarecrow is supposed to drive birds away _____ the garden.   _____

8. What time do you get home _____ school every day?   _____

9. Our team was playing _____ the team from the next town.   _____

10. He stuck the stamps _____ the envelope.   _____

11. This is an exception _____ the rule.   _____

12. He threw a stone and hit me _____ the eye.   _____

13. He took the child _____ the hand and helped her to cross the street.   _____

14. You can always depend _____ Rose.   _____

15. He asked the druggist to give him something _____ a headache.   _____

16. He doesn't understand a word _____ English.   _____

17. I met Catherine _____ my way to school.   _____

18. They laughed _____ the story I had told.   _____

19. The buses are always crowded _____ this time of day.   _____

20. The woman who waited _____ us was very polite.   _____

21. The package was too heavy _____ her to carry.   _____

22. He smiled _____ me in a very friendly way.   _____

23. We could see them _____ the distance.   _____

24. He was hiding _____ the tree.   _____

Select the correct form. Write your answer in the blank.

1. There (was, were) several students absent from class this morning.

   _____*were*_____

2. Angela (slept, was sleeping) when I called her.

   _____

3. We (are going, go) to school on the bus every morning.

   _____

4. He (is, has been) in the hospital for several weeks.

   _____

5. She is a very old friend of (me, my, mine).

   _____

6. I (am, was) going to call you, but I got home too late.

   _____

7. Look! Carlos (waits, is waiting) in line.

   _____

8. She said that she (can, could) speak French.

   _____

9. Martha's parents don't let (someone, anyone) call her after 9:30.

   _____

10. She works much harder (as, than) the other students.

    _____

11. She is (a, an) honest woman.

    _____

12. He is also (a, an) very honest person.

    _____

13. Where does he (lives, live)?

    _____

14. When I got there, they (had, were having) dinner.

    _____

15. He (said, told) that he would call me later.

    _____

16. She didn't think that she (can, could) go with us.

    _____

17. I thought that I (may, might) not be able to get there in time to see him.

    _____

18. Adela sent (her, to her) some beautiful flowers.

    _____

19. Hurry! The bus (comes, is coming) around the corner.

    _____

20. They (have, are having) their music lesson now.

    _____

21. They always (have, are having) their music lesson on Tuesday at this time.

    _____

22. They (spent, have spent) two months in Mexico last winter.

    _____

23. The teacher told (us, to us) the correct meaning of the word.

    _____

24. They (are, have been) very good friends for many years.

    _____

Review 2

Study and memorize the forms of these irregular verbs.

begin →	began →	begun	sing →	sang →	sung
drink →	drank →	drunk	sink →	sank →	sunk
ring →	rang →	rung	spring →	sprang →	sprung
shrink →	shrank →	shrunk	swim →	swam →	swum

These verbs have the same form for the present tense, the past tense, and the past participle. Study and memorize them.

bet	cut	let	shut
burst	hit	put	split
cost	hurt	set	spread

Write the correct form of the verb in parentheses.

1. The meeting had already (begin) when we arrived.   _____begun_____
2. We (sing) all the latest popular songs last night.   _____
3. The telephone (ring) just as I was leaving home.   _____
4. We (set) the table for dinner before we started cooking.   _____
5. Felipe (put) on his coat and left the room.   _____
6. It has (begin) to rain very hard.   _____
7. Has the school bell (ring) yet?   _____
8. Paolo (hurt) himself playing soccer yesterday.   _____
9. Mr. Wong has (drink) his medicine already.   _____
10. The teacher (let) us go home early yesterday.   _____
11. The ship had already (sink) when help arrived.   _____
12. Pina's dress (shrink) when she washed it.   _____
13. The cat (spring) upon the mouse and killed it instantly.   _____
14. We went to the beach yesterday and (swim) in the ocean for several hours.   _____
15. Have you ever (cut) yourself badly with a knife?   _____
16. The boy threw a stone at his companion and (hit) him in the eye.   _____
17. The news of the explosion last night (spread) quickly.   _____
18. It has (cost) her a great deal of money to educate her five children.   _____

Supposed to, used with the simple form of the main verb, expresses anticipation, expectation, or obligation. It is preceded by *to be* in either the past or present tense.

> Julia *is supposed to* get there before the weekend. (present)
>
> We *were supposed to* mail you the package last week, but we just mailed it today. (past)

Write the correct form of supposed to. *Include the verb in parentheses in your answer.*

1. We (spend) two hours on our homework every night.   _____are supposed to spend_____

2. He (leave) for Chicago last night, but he was delayed.   _____

3. I (arrive) at school every day at nine o'clock.   _____

4. Maria (be) here now.   _____

5. We (go) to Florida next week.   _____

6. Everyone (bring) a friend to the meeting tomorrow.   _____

7. She (telephone) me yesterday, but apparently she forgot.   _____

8. We (write) a composition for tomorrow's class.   _____

9. The maid (clean) this room every day.   _____

10. Their plane (arrive) two hours ago.   _____

11. Patrick (be) in Paris next month.   _____

12. The plane (leave) last night at midnight, but bad weather delayed it.   _____

13. They (deliver) the packages yesterday.   _____

14. She (send) me an e-mail message last night.   _____

15. This building (be) open to the public every day.   _____

16. June (leave) for Chicago next Wednesday.   _____

17. She (stay) there for about two weeks and then go on to California.   _____

USED TO

Used to describes an action that was a habit in the past, or an action that occurred often in the past but doesn't happen at the present time. It can also describe a state in the past.

> I *used to* run two miles a day. (Now I only run three times a week).
>
> We *used to* live in Paris. (Now we live in California).

A. *Write the phrase* used to *followed by the verb in parentheses.*

1. I (play) tennis well when I was taking lessons.   _used to play_

2. They (live) across the street from us.   _____

3. She and I (be) good friends.   _____

4. We (walk) to school together every day.   _____

5. He (work) for my father.   _____

6. She (be) one of the smartest girls in town.   _____

7. They (visit) us every summer.   _____

8. He (go) to Taiwan quite often.   _____

9. She (study) in our group.   _____

10. He (be) a teacher before he went into business.   _____

B. *Substitute a verb phrase with* used to *for the verb in italics.*

1. He *spent* too much time studying.   _used to spend_

2. She *visited* us.   _____

3. He *played* the violin well.   _____

4. She *sent* her mother flowers.   _____

5. He *wrote* articles for the newspapers.   _____

6. I *caught* cold when I went out in the rain.   _____

7. She *helped* me with my lessons.   _____

8. We *danced* until dawn.   _____

9. She *took* Grace to school.   _____

10. I *walked* two miles to school.   _____

Short answers are the most common form of answering direct questions. (They are also considered more polite than a simple yes or no answer.) A short answer consists of the subject of the sentence and an auxiliary verb or form of *to be*.

Can you play tennis?	Yes, I can.	No, I can't.
Do you know my friend?	Yes, I do.	No, I don't.
Is she at home?	Yes, she is.	No, she isn't.
Did Henry call you?	Yes, he did.	No, he didn't.

Note that pronouns replace the noun when the short answer is used.

Write affirmative and negative short answers for the questions. Answer singular you *questions with* I, *and answer plural* you *questions with* we.

1. Did you do your homework last night?   Yes, I did.   No, I didn't.

2. Is the sun shining?   _____   _____

3. Did it rain hard last night?   _____   _____

4. Is Alice a good teacher?   _____   _____

5. Have you and Will ever been to Mexico?   _____   _____

6. Can Mercedes play tennis well?   _____   _____

7. Does it often rain during April?   _____   _____

8. Is Roger supposed to be here now?   _____   _____

9. Have you and Nora had your dinner yet?   _____   _____

10. Will you be in class tomorrow?   _____   _____

11. Are you going to the movies tonight?   _____   _____

12. Does Christine speak English well?   _____   _____

13. Were you late for your lesson?   _____   _____

14. Was Adela always such a good student?   _____   _____

TAG QUESTIONS 1

With Affirmative Statements

Tag questions invite confirmation of a statement. They contain an auxiliary verb and a pronoun. Affirmative tag questions are used after negative statements; negative tag questions are used after affirmative statements.

> You live in the city, *don't you*?
>
> They had a long trip, *didn't they*?
>
> You will be at the dinner, *won't you*?
>
> Maria can speak Spanish, *can't she*?

In *there is/are* statements, treat *there* like a subject.

Add the correct tag question to the sentence.

1. Mario left for Rome last night, _____?   _____*didn't he*_____

2. She is a very good lawyer, _____?   _____

3. There are many students absent today, _____?   _____

4. You signed those documents, _____?   _____

5. The traffic will be very heavy, _____?   _____

6. Ana can help us, _____?   _____

7. It was a good movie, _____?   _____

8. He has been your teacher for a long time, _____?   _____

9. He is a very nice person, _____?   _____

10. That dog is yours, _____?   _____

11. The bus stops on this corner, _____?   _____

12. You gave me my change, _____?   _____

13. I paid you, _____?   _____

14. Angela is an excellent teacher, _____?   _____

15. She has studied English for many years, _____?   _____

16. Your father is an engineer, _____?   _____

17. You will be in class tomorrow, _____?   _____

18. It was raining at the time, _____?   _____

19. He is supposed to leave tomorrow, _____?   _____

20. You have had your lunch, _____?   _____

With Negative Statements

Remember that affirmative tag questions are used after negative statements.

> You don't live in the city, *do you*?
>
> They didn't have a long trip, *did they*?
>
> You won't be at the dinner, *will you*?
>
> Maria can't speak Spanish, *can she*?

Add the correct tag question to the sentence.

1. The plane didn't arrive on time, _____?   *did it*
2. The bus doesn't stop on this corner, _____?   _____
3. He is not a very dependable person, _____?   _____
4. Norma can't go with us, _____?   _____
5. You won't be back before noon, _____?   _____
6. It wasn't snowing at the time, _____?   _____
7. You haven't had your dinner yet, _____?   _____
8. His wife didn't come with him, _____?   _____
9. You can't speak French, _____?   _____
10. You don't know how to swim, _____?   _____
11. He doesn't like to go to the beach, _____?   _____
12. She won't be able to go with us, _____?   _____
13. You haven't ever been to Korea, _____?   _____
14. It hasn't begun to rain, _____?   _____
15. Your roof doesn't leak, _____?   _____
16. You weren't driving fast at the time, _____?   _____
17. Marcella wasn't hurt badly in the accident, _____? _____
18. The mail hasn't been delivered yet, _____?   _____
19. It hasn't rained hard in a long time, _____?   _____
20. You won't mention this to anyone, _____?   _____

TAG QUESTIONS 3

Review

Add the correct tag question to the sentence.

1. She always goes to New York by plane, _____?   _____*doesn't she*_____
2. Today isn't Wednesday, _____?   _____
3. His father is a well-known lawyer, _____?   _____
4. You saw that movie, _____?   _____
5. He won't be back until Wednesday, _____?   _____
6. It rains a lot during the month of April, _____?   _____
7. They have a very pretty home, _____?   _____
8. She is a surgeon, _____?   _____
9. You'll be in class tomorrow, _____?   _____
10. Your watch has stopped, _____?   _____
11. I paid you the money I owed you, _____?   _____
12. Bill hasn't been here today, _____?   _____
13. He didn't call you, _____?   _____
14. She dances very well, _____?   _____
15. They have already left for Tokyo, _____?   _____
16. You spoke to Sue about that matter, _____?   _____
17. She can meet us after the lesson, _____?   _____
18. He promised to be here at noon, _____?   _____
19. You haven't had your lunch yet, _____?   _____
20. The car skidded, _____?   _____
21. But it was the driver's fault, _____?   _____
22. You see him every weekend, _____?   _____
23. It has been a beautiful day, _____?   _____
24. He never mentioned it again, _____?   _____
25. She doesn't like to go to the beach, _____?   _____

A gerund is the form of a verb that is used as a noun and ends in *ing*. Certain verbs, like *enjoy, mind, stop, consider, appreciate,* and *finish,* can be followed by gerunds but not by infinitives.

> I don't mind *asking* for help.
>
> They have finished *painting*.
>
> She enjoys *swimming*.

Write the gerund form of the verb in parentheses.

1. We appreciate (hear) from you.   *hearing*

2. The man denied (take) the money.   _____

3. We cannot risk (invest) so much money.   _____

4. The driver could not avoid (hit) the curb.   _____

5. We are considering (move) to Miami.   _____

6. They have already finished (eat).   _____

7. We both enjoy (dance) very much.   _____

8. Do you mind (come) back later?   _____

9. He admitted (hide) the money.   _____

10. She says she doesn't mind (wait) for us.   _____

11. Steve and Tom have stopped (speak) to each other.   _____

12. We enjoy (listen) to music.   _____

13. He is going to stop (study) English.   _____

14. We will enjoy (use) your cottage at the beach while you are away.   _____

15. They have finally finished (paint) our apartment.   _____

16. Would you mind (open) the window?   _____

17. She denied (change) the address on the package.   _____

18. Sarah considered (borrow) some money.   _____

19. We would appreciate (receive) your answer immediately.   _____

20. He finally admitted (make) the mistake.   _____

21. My grandfather quit (work) a month ago.   _____

85

The following verbs may be followed by both gerunds and infinitives:

begin	hate	like	neglect	start
continue	intend	love	prefer	try

Complete the sentence, first with the gerund and then with the infinitive.

1. She loves (work) for herself. ___working___ ___to work___
2. He intends (leave) tomorrow. _____ _____
3. She will try (study) in the library. _____ _____
4. They will start (work) there next week. _____ _____
5. She hates (do) secretarial work. _____ _____
6. She will continue (work) in that same office until June. _____ _____
7. He prefers (dance) with his wife. _____ _____
8. I neglected (mention) it to Bill. _____ _____
9. He likes (teach) English to foreign students. _____ _____
10. They will begin (build) their new home soon. _____ _____
11. He prefers (watch) TV. _____ _____
12. She intends (stay) right where she is. _____ _____
13. He loves (criticize) others. _____ _____
14. We tried (find) an apartment near the park. _____ _____
15. They have finally started (speak) to each other. _____ _____
16. Rose loves (do) that kind of work. _____ _____
17. They continue (send) us a bill for the work. _____ _____
18. She tried (start) the car. _____ _____
19. I hadn't intended (make) you wait so long. _____ _____

Gerunds may be used after most prepositions in the same way as nouns.

> I am fond of *hiking*.
>
> You use this lever for *turning* on the heat.

Gerunds are used after the expressions *to be worth*, *no use*, and *do you mind*.

> Your ideas *are* certainly *worth considering*.
>
> It's *no use worrying* about it. It doesn't affect us.
>
> *Do you mind closing* the window? I'm cold.

Write the correct preposition and the gerund form of the verb in parentheses.

1. We are thinking (move) to Miami.   *of moving*
2. She got tired (wait) for her.   _____
3. We are both very fond (dance).   _____
4. He insisted (go) with us.   _____
5. There is no chance (see) him today.   _____
6. We are excited (go) to the Amazon.   _____
7. It is a question (find) a good teacher.   _____
8. We all need more lessons (speak).   _____
9. We are looking forward (see) you again.   _____
10. She has had no instruction (teach).   _____
11. He takes great pleasure (help) others.   _____
12. She insisted (help) me.   _____
13. He has no intention (leave) the class.   _____
14. We are all interested (learn) English.   _____
15. Are you fond (swim)?   _____
16. We were finally successful (locate) him.   _____
17. We get tired (study) the same thing.   _____
18. We are thinking (buy) a new car.   _____
19. We had no difficulty (find) where they lived.   _____
20. She has a talent (manage) children.   _____

IRREGULAR VERBS

Review 3

Write the correct form of the verb in parentheses.

1. It has (begin) to rain very hard.   *begun*

2. That dog has (bite) several people.   _____

3. The teacher (let) us go home early yesterday.   _____

4. All the birds have (fly) south for the winter.   _____

5. At our club meeting last night, we (choose) Rolando as our new president.   _____

6. Tom has (wear) that same hat for several years.   _____

7. While skating in the park yesterday, Henry (fall) and hurt himself.   _____

8. I have (give) them all the help I can.   _____

9. I caught my coat on a nail and (tear) it.   _____

10. I was born in Pennsylvania but (grow) up in New York.   _____

11. The boy ran and (hide) behind a tree.   _____

12. I have (know) Suzanne for many years.   _____

13. We have (drive) to Florida several times.   _____

14. We have already (sing) every old song we know.   _____

15. I stayed home last night and (write) some letters.   _____

16. During that storm last week, the wind (blow) down several trees on our block.   _____

17. We have (eat) in that restaurant several times.   _____

18. The police have not yet (find) out who stole the money.   _____

19. Our guide (lead) us through one government building after another yesterday.   _____

20. The dog has (lie) in that same spot all morning.   _____

21. I hope that you have not (throw) away those magazines I left here.   _____

22. The news about yesterday's accident (spread) quickly.   _____

23. The lake (freeze) over last week.   _____

24. They have not (speak) to each other in weeks.   _____

Select the correct form. Write your answer in the blank.

1. To *look for* something is to (appreciate it, search for it, overlook it, look it up).

   _____*search for it*_____

2. If you go somewhere *for good*, you go there (for health reasons, to look for work, frequently, permanently).

   _____

3. To *get on* a train is to (leave, board, inspect, walk through) it.

   _____

4. To *call up* someone is to (wave to, criticize, respect, telephone) him or her.

   _____

5. To *call on* someone is to (abuse, look down upon, visit, telephone) him or her.

   _____

6. To *call for* someone is to (look up to, come for, name, send for) him or her.

   _____

7. *I'd sooner study* means that I (dislike, hope, intend, prefer) to study.

   _____

8. To *talk over* something is to (overlook, forget, repeat, discuss) it.

   _____

9. To *look over* something is to (forget it, put it aside, examine it, postpone it).

   _____

10. To be *about to do* something is to be (worried about doing, at the point of doing, opposed to doing) it.

    _____

11. To *throw something away* is to (break, preserve, discard, need) it.

    _____

12. *So far* means (not at all, up to the present, suddenly, almost).

    _____

13. To be *used to* something means to be (tired of, happy about, accustomed to, worried about) it.

    _____

14. To *make believe* is to (pretend, discuss, withdraw, argue).

    _____

15. To be *mixed up* is to be (annoyed, amused, confused, disappointed).

    _____

16. To learn something *by heart* is to learn it (quickly, slowly, carelessly, by memory).

    _____

17. If someone says to you, "Look out!" it means (look out the window, be careful, sit down and rest).

    _____

Words Used as Nouns and Verbs

Many words are used as both nouns and verbs, with no change in their form.

Noun	*Verb*
Their *work* is excellent.	They *work* here every day.
There is a *need* for world peace.	We *need* peace in the world.

Here are some of the many other English words that may be used as nouns and verbs without a change in form:

block	fall	kiss	play	shout	taste
call	finish	mark	point	smile	tie
crowd	fire	mind	present	start	time
cry	fish	mistake	rest	study	walk
curse	fool	move	result	surprise	watch
drink	guide	offer	ride	talk	wish
escape	help	part	scream		

If the word in italics is used as a noun, write noun; *if it is used as a verb, write* verb.

1. We *look* very elegant in our new clothes.   _____verb_____

   We saw the *look* of surprise on his face.   _____noun_____

2. It is a *question* of finding the right person for the job.   _____

   The police are going to *question* everyone about the robbery.   _____

3. There is no *need* to discuss the matter further.   _____

   We *need* some new tires for our car.   _____

4. All children *love* candy.   _____

   His *love* for her will never die.   _____

5. The *sound* of the shot was heard by everyone.   _____

   Both men *sound* angry to me.   _____

6. Martha's *face* looked pale and drawn.   _____

   All the buildings on our block *face* the park.   _____

7. She *plans* to go to Australia in June.   _____

   Their *plans* to go to Australia in June fell through.   _____

8. Did you *notice* the new dress Joyce was wearing?   _____

   Each teacher received a *notice* of the change in exam dates.   _____

Many words have different, though similar or related, forms as nouns and verbs. Study and memorize the differences as you write the corresponding noun form of the verb.

1.	to decide	_decision_	23.	to appear	_____
2.	to excite	_excitement_	24.	to believe	_____
3.	to weigh	_____	25.	to breathe	_____
4.	to oblige	_____	26.	to confuse	_____
5.	to recognize	_____	27.	to inspect	_____
6.	to insist	_____	28.	to admire	_____
7.	to repeat	_____	29.	to relieve	_____
8.	to locate	_____	30.	to choose	_____
9.	to arrive	_____	31.	to embarrass	_____
10.	to analyze	_____	32.	to destroy	_____
11.	to tempt	_____	33.	to complete	_____
12.	to argue	_____	34.	to satisfy	_____
13.	to adjust	_____	35.	to enjoy	_____
14.	to react	_____	36.	to hesitate	_____
15.	to expect	_____	37.	to paralyze	_____
16.	to prove	_____	38.	to identity	_____
17.	to describe	_____	39.	to protect	_____
18.	to arrange	_____	40.	to obey	_____
19.	to treat	_____	41.	to discover	_____
20.	to consider	_____	42.	to complain	_____
21.	to explain	_____	43.	to criticize	_____
22.	to annoy	_____	44.	to refuse	_____

NOUN AND VERB FORMS 2

Write the corresponding verb form of the noun.

1. imagination   *to imagine*
2. existence   *to exist*
3. growth _____
4. interference _____
5. burial _____
6. explosion _____
7. interruption _____
8. disturbance _____
9. apology _____
10. admission _____
11. repetition _____
12. proof _____
13. collection _____
14. relief _____
15. impression _____
16. marriage _____
17. denial _____
18. intention _____
19. choice _____
20. approval _____
21. advice _____
22. death _____
23. suspicion _____
24. agreement _____

25. amusement _____
26. excitement _____
27. robbery _____
28. success _____
29. punishment _____
30. decision _____
31. observation _____
32. reservation _____
33. adoption _____
34. deception _____
35. remainder _____
36. loss _____
37. failure _____
38. warning _____
39. entrance _____
40. beginning _____
41. withdrawal _____
42. paralysis _____
43. belief _____
44. conclusion _____
45. refusal _____
46. destruction _____
47. criticism _____
48. complaint _____

Write the correct preposition in the blank.

1. She is not interested _____ learning English.   _____ *in* _____

2. He is worried _____ his wife's health.   _____

3. It is a question _____ getting permission from the authorities.   _____

4. She insisted _____ helping me with the work.   _____

5. For tomorrow's lesson, we will study from page ten _____ page
    fifteen.   _____

6. He poured the wine _____ the glass.   _____

7. The button fell _____ his shirt.   _____

8. She said that, _____ the circumstances, she could do nothing
    for us.   _____

9. He didn't mention anything to me _____ it.   _____

10. We have been waiting for him _____ twenty minutes.   _____

11. Paris is famous _____ its many art galleries.   _____

12. I didn't interfere _____ his plans.   _____

13. Don't lean _____ that fence; it's just been painted.   _____

14. I mistook Jane _____ her sister.   _____

15. I want to ask a favor _____ you.   _____

16. He was absent _____ class yesterday.   _____

17. Don't drink _____ that glass.   _____

18. Her English is improving little _____ little.   _____

19. Who will take care _____ your dog while you are away?   _____

20. She should go _____ a diet.   _____

21. His face is very familiar _____ me.   _____

22. We'll have to postpone our trip _____ next month.   _____

23. The game was called off because _____ rain.   _____

24. Are you waiting _____ someone?   _____

25. Take the dog out _____ a walk.   _____

Select the correct form. Write your answer in the blank.

1. He insisted (to go, on going) with us.   *on going*

2. They are thinking (to move, of moving) to Oakland. _____

3. We (have lived, lived) in this same apartment since June. _____

4. She is not interested (to learn, in learning) English. _____

5. Do you mind (to wait, waiting) a few minutes? _____

6. We would appreciate (to hear, hearing) from you as soon as possible. _____

7. They have finally finished (to paint, painting) our apartment. _____

8. Listen! The train (comes, is coming). _____

9. The baby (cries, is crying) frequently during the day. _____

10. When I got up this morning, it (rained, was raining) hard. _____

11. I am used to (study, studying) with Ms. Levine, and I don't want to change to another teacher. _____

12. Their plane (supposed, is supposed) to arrive at midnight. _____

13. He asked (that I go, me to go) with him. _____

14. She is an old friend of (us, our, ours). _____

15. The ship had already (sank, sunk) when help arrived. _____

16. He asked me what time it (is, was). _____

17. She said that she (can, could) not speak English well. _____

18. He might (leave, leaves) class early today. _____

19. I couldn't find my book (somewhere, anywhere). _____

20. She (works, has worked) in that office for many years. _____

21. He (studied, has studied) English for two years when he was in high school. _____

22. When we arrived, they (watched, were watching) TV. _____

23. There's no use (complaining, to complain) about the weather. _____

24. (Someone, Anyone) called on you yesterday. _____

25. I (wanted, had wanted) twins before I realized how much work children are. _____

Questions in indirect speech are expressed as statements.

> **Direct: Tamara asked, "Where *does* Sean *live*?"**
>
> **Indirect: Tamara asked where Sean *lived*.**

When the direct question does not contain a question word, the indirect question requires the introduction of *if* or *whether*.

> **Direct: Tamara asked, "Does Sean live here?"**
>
> **Indirect: Tamara asked *if* Sean lived here.**
>
> **Indirect: Tamara asked *whether* Sean lived here.**

Select the correct form. Write your answer in the blank.

1. She asked me what time (was it, it was). _____*it was*_____

2. I'll tell you what time (is it, it is). _____

3. He wanted to know how old (I was, was I). _____

4. She asked me when (would I, I would) return. _____

5. Ask him what time (is it, it is). _____

6. Tell her how old (are you, you are). _____

7. Ask him why (was he, he was) late. _____

8. I don't know where (does she live, she lives). _____

9. He didn't tell me where (did she live, she lived). _____

10. The teacher asked me where (was I, I was) going. _____

11. I don't know how far (is it, it is) from here to Seville. _____

12. She asked me how much (did I pay, I paid) for my car. _____

13. Ask Marc where (is he, he is) going. _____

14. Sheila asked me how (did I like, I liked) my new class. _____

15. I don't know where (did Adam put, Adam put) all those old magazines. _____

16. No one seems to know where (did she go, she went). _____

17. I forget where (did I put, I put) it. _____

18. He asked us in which room (we had, did we have) our English lesson. _____

SHOULD, OUGHT TO

Should and *ought to* mean the same thing. They both express obligation. In negative statements, the contracted form *shouldn't* is normally used.

> You *should spend* more time with your family.
>
> You *ought to spend* more time with your family.
>
> She *shouldn't (should not) buy* so much.
>
> She *ought not to buy* so much. (not common)

Should and *ought* are less strong in meaning than *must*. *Must* has almost the force of a command. *Should* and *ought to* suggest an obligation to do a certain thing.

Substitute ought to *for* should *in the sentence. Write the complete verb.*

1. She *should attend* class more regularly. *ought to attend*
2. I *should go* to bed earlier every night. _____
3. He *should choose* his friends more carefully. _____
4. She *should not talk* back to her parents. _____
5. You *should not write* your compositions in pencil. _____
6. She *should be* more careful of her health. _____
7. They *should try* to arrive at school on time. _____
8. We *should get* more physical exercise. _____
9. She *should have* more respect for her parents. _____
10. She *should not speak* to him in that way. _____
11. Children *should obey* their parents. _____
12. Rod *should not read* so much. _____
13. I *should write* to my friends more often. _____
14. He *should try* to put on some weight. _____
15. They *should take* their studies more seriously. _____
16. We *should go* home by bus instead of taxi. _____
17. This letter *should be sent* at once. _____
18. They *should arrive* at five o'clock. _____
19. Regina *should sign* these documents right away. _____
20. He *should not spend* so much money. _____

Form the past of sentences with *should* and *ought to* by using *have* and the past participle of the main verb.

> We *should be* more careful.
>
> We *should have been* more careful.
>
> He *ought to finish* his work quickly.
>
> He *ought to have finished* his work quickly.

Note that the past form of *should* and *ought to* has a negative feeling, since it suggests that something should have been done but was not done.

Change the sentence to the past form.

1. Al *should study* more before his exams.   *should have studied*

2. You *should go* with me to visit them.   _____

3. They *should arrive* at five o'clock.   _____

4. You *should go* by plane.   _____

5. She *should call* you more often.   _____

6. This letter *should be sent* at once.   _____

7. This package *should be delivered* immediately.   _____

8. She *should be* more careful in handling such things.   _____

9. You *should tell* me about it.   _____

10. He *should go* to see a doctor right away.   _____

11. The director *should read* this letter.   _____

12. He *should visit* us more often.   _____

13. You *should call* the police.   _____

14. She *should spend* less money.   _____

15. He *should spend* more time on his homework.   _____

16. They *should finish* that work today.   _____

17. She *should be* more careful of her health.   _____

18. They *should tell* no one about it.   _____

19. She *should ask* permission first.   _____

20. He *should practice* his English more.   _____

SHOULD, OUGHT TO

Past Form 2

Change the sentence to the past tense. Remember to change the simple form of the verb to the perfect form.

1. She *ought to study* much harder.   _ought to have studied_
2. You *ought to go* with me to visit them.   _____
3. He *ought to travel* by plane.   _____
4. We *ought to save* more money.   _____
5. She *ought to be* more careful of her health.   _____
6. He *ought to sign* these letters at once.   _____
7. This package *ought to be sent* by express mail.   _____
8. She *ought to arrive* earlier.   _____
9. This package *ought to be delivered* right away.   _____
10. These letters *ought to be faxed*.   _____
11. He *ought to see* a doctor at once.   _____
12. They *ought to make* reservations early.   _____
13. We *ought not to waste* so much valuable time.   _____
14. You *ought to explain* it to her more carefully.   _____
15. We *ought to telephone* him at once.   _____
16. She *ought to work* harder.   _____
17. This material *ought to be prepared* right away.   _____
18. We *ought to telephone* the police.   _____
19. She *ought to get* more rest.   _____
20. You *ought to go* to bed earlier every night.   _____
21. She *ought to write* to her parents more often.   _____
22. These chairs *ought to be put* in the other room.   _____

A conditional sentence has two clauses: the dependent clause introduced by *if* (also called the *if* clause) and the main, or result, clause.

> **If you study, you will pass your exam.**
>
> **If you lend me five dollars, I will pay you back tomorrow.**

In future real conditional sentences, the *if* clause is in the present tense, and the result clause is in the future tense. The modals *can, may,* or *might* may also be used in the main clause.

Write the correct form of the verb in parentheses in order to complete the conditional sentence.

1. If Beatrice (study) hard, she will surely graduate.   *studies*

2. If he (work) hard, he will pass his exam.   _____

3. If she (hurry), she will be able to go with us.   _____

4. If it (rain), we will not go to the beach.   _____

5. If Randy (come), he can help us.   _____

6. If you (attend) class regularly, you will learn English quickly.   _____

7. If the weather (be) nice tomorrow, we will go to the beach.   _____

8. If he (call) me, I will let you know.   _____

9. If I (see) her, I will give her your message.   _____

10. If it (not rain), we will go on a picnic tomorrow.   _____

11. If I (have) time, I will call you tonight.   _____

12. If they (leave) early, they can get there on time.   _____

13. If she (get) back before four, I will call you.   _____

14. If Colette (call), I will tell her about our plans.   _____

15. If he (not come), I don't know what we will do.   _____

16. If we (decide) to go swimming, we will give you a ring.   _____

17. If the weather (get) any colder, we will have to buy overcoats.   _____

18. If the dog (bite) him, he will have to go to the hospital.   _____

19. If you (have) time tomorrow, we can go to the ball game.   _____

CONDITIONAL SENTENCES

Future Real 2

Write the correct form of the verb in parentheses in order to complete the future real conditional sentence.

1. If Sue studies hard, she (pass) her examination.   <u>will pass</u>

2. If I have time tomorrow, I (visit) you.   _____

3. If he doesn't hurry, we (miss) our train.   _____

4. If the weather is good next week, we probably (go) hunting.   _____

5. If it doesn't rain tomorrow, we (go) to the beach.   _____

6. If you attend class regularly, you (learn) English quickly.   _____

7. If they leave early enough, they (be) able to get tickets.   _____

8. If Ann calls, I (tell) her about our change in plans.   _____

9. If we decide to go to the beach, I (let) you know.   _____

10. If it snows tonight, we (have) to stay at home all day tomorrow.   _____

11. If the weather continues to be so cold, I (have) to buy some warmer clothing.   _____

12. If I get a good grade on my exam, my parents (be) pleased.   _____

13. If I have time, I (give) you a ring tomorrow.   _____

14. If I have a car next summer, I (drive) to the beach every day.   _____

15. If we have enough money, we (take) a trip abroad next summer.   _____

16. If he works hard, he (earn) a lot of money in that job.   _____

17. If they get married now, they (have) to live with his parents.   _____

18. If Stella comes before I leave, I (explain) everything to her.   _____

19. If you go to bed earlier, you (be) less tired.   _____

20. If you practice every day, you (play) the piano well.   _____

In present unreal conditional sentences, the *if* clause is in the past tense, and the result clause takes *would, could,* or *might.* In the negative form, the contracted forms (*didn't, wouldn't,* etc.) are generally used. This kind of conditional sentence is used to talk about a situation that is purely hypothetical.

> If it *snowed* in the middle of the summer, all the flowers *would die.*
>
> If Joseph *studied* harder, he *wouldn't fail* all his exams.
>
> If I *didn't have* a car, I *would ride* the bus.

Write the correct form of the verb in order to complete the present unreal conditional sentence. Use the contracted form for negative sentences.

1. If Stan (spend) more time on his lessons, he would get better grades. _____ *spent* _____

2. If I (have) more time, I would go to the beach every day. _____

3. If I (own) a car, I would take a trip to California. _____

4. If she (work) harder, she would get a better position. _____

5. If I (know) his telephone number, I would call him up. _____

6. If I (speak) French well, I would take a trip to France. _____

7. If she (go) to bed earlier, she wouldn't be so tired. _____

8. If he (pay) more attention in class, he would pass the course. _____

9. If I (know) how to drive, I would buy a car. _____

10. If we (study) together, we could prepare our homework more easily. _____

11. If she (like) languages, it would be easier for her to learn. _____

12. If they (have) more conversation practice, they would speak better. _____

13. If we (have) more time, we would make more progress. _____

14. If I (not have) to work tomorrow, I would go to the beach with you. _____

15. If he (not waste) so much time in class, he would make more progress. _____

CONDITIONAL SENTENCES

Present Unreal 2

Write the correct form of the verb in order to complete the present unreal conditional sentence.

1. If Marcia studied harder, she (pass) her exams easily.   *would pass*

2. If I knew how to play the piano, I (play) for my friends
    every night.   _____

3. If I didn't have to work today, I (go) swimming in our pool.   _____

4. If Tom had more practice in conversation, he (speak) English
    much better.   _____

5. If she knew how to drive well, she (have) fewer accidents.   _____

6. If I liked languages better, I (study) French as well as English. _____

7. If Randy had the time, he (go) to Mexico with us.   _____

8. If she spent more time on her homework, she (get) better
    grades.   _____

9. If we studied together, we (make) more progress.   _____

10. If I had a car, I (take) a trip to Miami.   _____

11. If it didn't cost so much, I (go) to Europe on my next vacation. _____

12. If I didn't live so far away, I (walk) to school every day.   _____

13. If I had the money, I (buy) some new clothes.   _____

14. If I knew her better, I (ask) her to go with us.   _____

15. If I had the money, I (give) it to you gladly.   _____

16. If I had a good book to read, I (stay) at home tonight
    and read it.   _____

17. If we left right away, we (be) there by two o'clock.   _____

18. If I had a car, I (not ride) the bus.   _____

In present unreal conditional sentences, the correct form of *to be* is *were* in all persons in the *if* clause.

> If I *were* in your place, I wouldn't argue with the police officer.
>
> If you *were* taller, we could dance better.
>
> If he *were* smart, he wouldn't say a word.

Write the correct form of the verb in order to complete the present unreal conditional sentence.

1. If I (be) in your position, I wouldn't go with him.   *were*

2. If today (be) Saturday, I wouldn't have to work.   _____

3. If the weather (be) warmer, we could go to the beach.   _____

4. If he (be) a friend of mine, I would ask him about it.   _____

5. If I (be) not so busy today, I would go fishing with you.   _____

6. If I (be) a millionaire, I would spend every winter in Miami.   _____

7. If Alan (be) here now, we could ask him about it.   _____

8. If Sue (be) more intelligent, she would never say such a thing.   _____

9. If I (be) not so tired tonight, I would go to the movies with you.   _____

10. If today (be) a holiday, we could all go on a picnic.   _____

11. If I were you, I (explain) everything to him.   _____

12. If Patricia were only here now, she (know) how to handle this matter.   _____

13. If today were a holiday, we (go) to the beach.   _____

14. If I were not so busy, I (go) with you.   _____

15. If you were a millionaire, you (not work) so hard.   _____

16. If she were more ambitious, she (not be) content with such a low-paying job.   _____

17. If I were in your position, I (continue) to study English for several years more.   _____

18. If she were my boss, I (ask) her for a raise.   _____

19. If you were here, we (not need) a telephone.   _____

CONDITIONAL SENTENCES

Past Unreal 1

In past unreal conditional sentences, the *if* clause is in the past perfect tense, and the result clause uses *would have, could have,* or *might have.*

> If you *had studied*, you *would have (would've) passed* the exam.
>
> If I *had known,* I *wouldn't have said* anything.

Write the correct form of the verb in order to complete the past unreal conditional sentence.

1. If he (study) more, he would have passed his exam. _had studied_

2. If I (know) you were waiting for me, I would have hurried to get here. _____

3. If you (call) me, I would have waited for you. _____

4. If the weather yesterday (be) nice, we would have gone to the beach. _____

5. If yesterday (be) a holiday, the stores would all have been closed. _____

6. If you (go) with us, you would have seen a good show. _____

7. If she (tell) me the truth, I would have been less angry. _____

8. If I (receive) an invitation, I would have gone with you to the party. _____

9. If he (had) enough money, he would have bought a new car. _____

10. If I (think) about it in time, I would have asked Giselle to go with us. _____

11. If I (see) him, I would have given him your message. _____

12. If it (not rain) so hard, we would have been able to make the trip. _____

13. If she (leave) in time, she would have caught the train. _____

14. If I (take) a taxi, I would not have missed him. _____

15. If you (call) me, I would have been glad to go with you. _____

16. If I (know) about this yesterday, I could have brought the money with me. _____

Write the correct form of the verb in order to complete the past unreal conditional sentence. Use contracted forms where appropriate.

1. If Saul had studied harder, he (pass) his examinations.   <u>would have passed</u>

2. If I had had your telephone number, I (call) you.   _____

3. If yesterday had been a holiday, we (go) to the beach.   _____

4. If I had known about this last night, I (act) differently.   _____

5. If he had attended class more regularly, he (get) a better grade.   _____

6. If they had left earlier, they (catch) the train.   _____

7. If I had been in your place, I (refuse) to give him the money.   _____

8. If I had seen her, I (give) her your message.   _____

9. If they had come on time, I (talk) with them.   _____

10. If she had had more experience, she (get) the job.   _____

11. If she had paid more attention in class, she (do) better on her examination.   _____

12. If they had invited me, I (go) with them.   _____

13. If I had had the money, I (buy) that car.   _____

14. If she had acted differently, we (take) her along.   _____

15. If I had been in your position, I (go) with them.   _____

16. If you had gone with us, you (meet) her.   _____

17. If I had had a car last summer, I (drive) to California.   _____

18. If it had not rained, we (go) on a picnic yesterday.   _____

19. If you had come earlier, you (have) a fine dinner.   _____

20. If she had told me the truth, I (be) less angry.   _____

21. If I had known it was going to rain, I (take) my umbrella.   _____

22. If we had hurried, we (get) there in time.   _____

WISH

Wish suggests a situation that is unreal. After *wish*, use a past tense clause to suggest present action and a past perfect tense clause to suggest past action.

> I wish I *knew* what to do in this situation. (present)
>
> I wish I *had known* what to do in that situation. (past)

Write the correct form of the verb in parentheses.

1. I wish I (know) how to swim.   *knew*

2. I wish I (go) with you to the opera last night. _____

3. Vanessa wishes she (speak) Dutch. _____

4. I wish I (have) a car. _____

5. I wish you (call) me about this yesterday. _____

6. I wish I (study) last night. _____

7. Harry wishes he (be) in his native country now. _____

8. I wish I (be) in Florida during this cold spell. _____

9. I wish today (be) Sunday. _____

10. I wish I (know) that you were going to the beach yesterday. _____

11. I wish I (start) to study English long ago. _____

12. I wish I (study) English with Michelle last year. _____

13. I wish I (know) English perfectly. _____

14. Kathy wishes she (have) today off. _____

15. Peter wishes he (be) an engineer instead of a doctor. _____

16. I wish I (have) today off. I would go swimming. _____

17. I wish I (have) yesterday off. I would have gone swimming. _____

18. I wish today (be) Saturday. I would not have to work, and I could go to the beach. _____

19. I wish yesterday (be) Saturday. I would not have had to work, and I could have gone to the beach. _____

20. I wish the weather (be) warm so that we could go to the park. _____

When a dependent clause introduced by *if* describes a future possibility, it uses the present tense. When dependent clauses introduced by *as long as, as soon as, before, unless, until, when,* and *while* describe a future condition, they also use the present tense.

> I'll see him *when* he *comes.*
>
> I'll see him *as soon as* he *comes.*
>
> I'll wait *until* he *arrives.*
>
> *While I'm* at the supermarket, I'll pick up a pasta salad.

Write the correct form of the verb in parentheses.

1. I will see him as soon as he (get) here.   _gets_
2. I will give it to her when she (arrive).   _____
3. Before I (leave), I will explain everything to him.   _____
4. We will leave as soon as Anita (get) here.   _____
5. Don't leave until I (let) you know.   _____
6. I won't go unless you (go), too.   _____
7. Wait right here until I (telephone) you.   _____
8. I'll let you know as soon as I (get) back.   _____
9. Don't call unless you (need) me badly.   _____
10. We'll have to wait here until the doctor (arrive).   _____
11. Keep an eye on my bag while I (get) my ticket.   _____
12. When the weather (get) warmer, you can go swimming.   _____
13. Give him my message as soon as you (see) him.   _____
14. Don't leave until Olga (get) back.   _____
15. Wait right here while I (call) them.   _____
16. I will wait here until the mail (arrive).   _____
17. Call me as soon as you (hear) from them.   _____
18. Wait here until Ted (come).   _____
19. We can tell her when she (return) from her trip.   _____
20. The program won't begin until the president (arrive).   _____

CAPITAL LETTERS

Capital letters are used for names of people (including their titles), places, businesses and institutions, publications, languages and nationalities, days of the week, months, and holidays:

People	Places	Businesses and Institutions
Mr. Robert Woodson	Moscow	Riverside Restaurant
Tom	Japan	State Bank
Dr. Sato	Central Park	The Museum of Art

Publications*	Languages and Nationalities	Days, Weeks, Months, and Holidays
Grammar to Go	Mexican	Thursday
The London Times	Chinese	November
Gone with the Wind	Greek	Thanksgiving

*In titles, a small word such as *a, the,* or *of* isn't normally capitalized unless it is the first word of the title.

A capital letter is always used at the beginning of a sentence and at the beginning of a direct quotation.

Add capital letters to the sentences.

1. we will celebrate our daughter's birthday next sunday.

   We will celebrate our daughter's birthday next Sunday.

2. they live across the street from riverside park.

3. sam speaks french as well as he speaks english.

4. our teacher, dr. gomez, is colombian.

5. we will celebrate new year's day in new york.

6. "there's a good program on TV tonight," said janet.

7. in mexico, independence day is celebrated in september.

8. have you ever read the famous russian novel *war and peace?*

Commas are used to:

separate items in a list

> **We brought sandwiches, salad, and coffee to the picnic.**
>
> **John got home, took off his shoes, and lay down for a nap.**

separate items in dates and geographical locations

> **My son was born on Tuesday, October 21, 2003, in Paris, France.**

separate direct quotations from the rest of the sentence

> **"I'm ready to go," said Ling.**
>
> **Ling said, "I'm ready to go."**

Add commas to the sentences.

1. Don't forget to feed the cat water the plants and pick up the mail.

   Don't forget to feed the cat, water the plants, and pick up the mail.

2. I studied in London England.

3. They arrived in Chicago Illinois on Friday May 3.

4. You need eggs flour sugar and milk to make a cake.

5. Beat the eggs first add the milk and stir in the flour.

6. The semester ends on Friday December 12.

7. "I'll call you later" said George.

8. Samantha asked "May I borrow your dictionary?"

9. We are moving our offices to Seattle Washington on Monday August 2.

Commas are used when two sentences are connected with *and* or *but*.

> John got home early, and he cooked dinner.
>
> I like ice cream, but I don't like cake.

When a sentence begins with a dependent clause, a comma is used to separate it from the main clause.

> If it rains, we won't go to the beach.
>
> When it started to snow, we went inside.

Commas are not used when the sentence begins with the main clause.

> We went inside when it started to snow.

Add commas to the sentences.

1. We bought a newspaper and we also bought some candy.

   We bought a newspaper, and we also bought some candy.

2. Although I was hungry all day I didn't eat until evening.

3. Before he got on the plane Roger called his office.

4. Henry cooked dinner but he didn't wash the dishes.

5. Ann will work in the garden and Ed will paint the fence if it doesn't rain tomorrow.

6. If I finish my homework before 8:00 I'll call you.

7. Although Carol works hard she doesn't make a lot of money.

8. By the time we arrived they had already left.

9. When the phone rang I was sleeping.

Add commas and capital letters to the sentences.

1. "our new neighbor's name is dr. lee" jane said.

   "Our new neighbor's name is Dr. Lee,"
   Jane said.

2. Although he was very busy robert offered to help jim.

3. "this is a beautiful neighborhood" said sara.

4. lisa replied "we enjoy living here very much."

5. anil has a car but he rarely drives it.

6. if you don't understand the lesson ask the teacher for help.

7. my birthday is on thursday but we will celebrate it on saturday.

8. john bought a ring a bracelet and some earrings for mary.

9. when you get home please walk the dog.

10. my favorite play by shakespeare is *romeo and juliet*.

11. i enjoyed *gone with the wind* but my sister didn't like it.

12. as soon as we get home we'll start preparing the food for our independence day picnic.

13. if i had more free time i would learn to play the piano.

Homophones are words that have the same pronunciation but different meanings.
Write the corresponding homophone for each word.

1.	their	*there*	26.	seem	_____
2.	weight	*wait*	27.	some	_____
3.	threw	_____	28.	hole	_____
4.	knew	_____	29.	higher	_____
5.	waist	_____	30.	him	_____
6.	way	_____	31.	meet	_____
7.	weak	_____	32.	made	_____
8.	wood	_____	33.	mail	_____
9.	knight	_____	34.	in	_____
10.	know	_____	35.	clothes	_____
11.	cell	_____	36.	our	_____
12.	cellar	_____	37.	break	_____
13.	cent	_____	38.	knot	_____
14.	scene	_____	39.	pear	_____
15.	forth	_____	40.	plane	_____
16.	die	_____	41.	piece	_____
17.	flour	_____	42.	buy	_____
18.	road	_____	43.	role	_____
19.	right	_____	44.	guessed	_____
20.	red	_____	45.	steal	_____
21.	sail	_____	46.	so	_____
22.	sees	_____	47.	son	_____
23.	berth	_____	48.	principle	_____
24.	heal	_____	49.	pail	_____
25.	hear	_____	50.	dear	_____

Many words form their opposites by taking a prefix. Write the opposite of the word by adding the necessary prefix.

1. happy   _unhappy_
2. legal   _illegal_
3. able _____
4. believable _____
5. regular _____
6. honest _____
7. (to) appear _____
8. (to) obey _____
9. (to) like _____
10. attractive _____
11. legible _____
12. (to) pronounce _____
13. (to) connect _____
14. (to) continue _____
15. (to) understand _____
16. (to) tie _____
17. (to) wrap _____
18. (to) button _____
19. advantage _____
20. mature _____
21. capable _____
22. organized _____
23. (to) dress _____
24. (to) fold _____

25. fortunate _____
26. fair _____
27. (to) agree _____
28. (to) approve _____
29. polite _____
30. discreet _____
31. correct _____
32. sincere _____
33. (to) cover _____
34. furnished _____
35. healthy _____
36. opened _____
37. armed _____
38. patient _____
39. accurate _____
40. (to) infect _____
41. (to) inherit _____
42. convenient _____
43. real _____
44. kind _____
45. satisfied _____
46. agreeable _____
47. pleasant _____
48. dependent _____

Write the correct preposition or particle in the blank.

1. The boys in the class like to play tricks _____ Tom. _____on_____

2. She never pays any attention _____ what the teacher says. _____

3. I think that he has fallen _____ love with Annie. _____

4. The senator insisted that he had had nothing to do _____ the scandal. _____

5. I see Jack once _____ a while in the school cafeteria. _____

6. I know several of Frost's poems _____ heart. _____

7. I have always been afraid _____ spiders and insects. _____

8. Sally apologized _____ breaking the window with a baseball. _____

9. I feel sorry _____ anyone who is as poor as he is. _____

10. Let's go _____ a movie. I don't feel like studying. _____

11. We are looking forward _____ her visit. _____

12. Peter insisted _____ helping me with my homework. _____

13. Because of his dark hair and eyes, everyone always takes Sam _____ my brother. _____

14. My son is very interested _____ dinosaurs right now. _____

15. My wallet fell out _____ my pocket while I was riding the bus. _____

16. The teacher always stands _____ front of the class. _____

17. She always insists _____ counting her change carefully. _____

18. My book is different _____ yours. _____

19. Sally has been a teacher in this school _____ 1998. _____

20. He has tried several times to borrow money _____ me. _____

21. When are you going _____ vacation? _____

22. She took the children _____ the zoo. _____

23. They traveled _____ plane. _____

24. They left the waiter's tip _____ the table. _____

25. This elevator is going _____. _____

Select the correct form. Write your answer in the blank.

1. He (said, told) me that his last name was Ortega.   *told*

2. He asked me where (was I, I was) going.   _____

3. Ronald said that he (will, would) be here before noon.   _____

4. You ought (to do, to have done) this work yesterday.   _____

5. If I (was, were) you, I wouldn't mention it to him.   _____

6. Call me as soon as Alice (arrives, will arrive).   _____

7. If I (saw, had seen) Rose yesterday, I would have given her your message.   _____

8. She wants to know where (do you live, you live).   _____

9. We are old friends of (them, theirs, their).   _____

10. You should (tell, have told) me about it yesterday.   _____

11. Listen! I think the telephone (rings, is ringing).   _____

12. Do you mind (to come, coming) back a little later?   _____

13. He insisted (on waiting, to wait) for me after the lesson.   _____

14. We had difficulty (in locating, to locate) him.   _____

15. The train (supposed, is supposed) to arrive at two o'clock.   _____

16. How long (do you study, have you studied) English?   _____

17. We have been friends (during, for) many years.   _____

18. Joan speaks Spanish (good, well).   _____

19. He is (a, an) very honest man.   _____

20. This is (a, an) easy exercise.   _____

21. They (live, have lived) in that house for many years.   _____

22. Ana always (comes, is coming) to school by bus.   _____

23. When you called, I (slept, was sleeping).   _____

24. You (should call, should have called) me last night.   _____

25. I didn't see (some, any) children in the park.   _____

ABBREVIATED CLAUSES

With *Too*

We avoid repeating earlier words and phrases in English by using an appropriate auxiliary verb and *too* in short affirmative clauses.

> Henry went to the movies, and I went to the movies.
>
> Henry went to the movies, and I *did, too*.
>
> I like New York, and Alice likes New York.
>
> I like New York, and Alice *does, too*.

Rewrite the words in italics using the correct auxiliary and too.

1. She studied English, and *I studied English.*   _____I did, too_____

2. She is going to New York, and *he is going to New York.*   _____

3. He knows Mr. Lee well, and *I know Mr. Lee well.*   _____

4. He used to live in Washington, and *his brother used to live in Washington.*   _____

5. I like to play computer games, and *she likes to play computer games.*   _____

6. She will be at the meeting, and *I will be at the meeting.*   _____

7. I had to work last night, and *Ed had to work last night.*   _____

8. I have seen that picture, and *she has seen that picture.*   _____

9. He was absent from class, and *his sister was absent from class.*   _____

10. We enjoyed the concert, and *they enjoyed the concert.*   _____

11. He is supposed to work tomorrow, and *I am supposed to work tomorrow.*   _____

12. She can speak French, and *he can speak French.*   _____

13. Tony has gone to the movies, and *Ann has gone to the movies.*   _____

14. He is making good progress, and *she is making good progress.*   _____

15. Sean gets a lot of e-mail, and *I get a lot of e-mail.*   _____

16. He studies hard, and *his sister studies hard.*   _____

17. You will be late, and *I will be late.*   _____

18. He walks slowly, and *you walk slowly.*   _____

19. She may go, and *I may go.*   _____

We can also avoid repeating earlier words and phrases by using an appropriate auxiliary verb and *so*. Note that when we use *so*, the auxiliary precedes the subject.

> Henry went to the movies, and I went to the movies.
>
> Henry went to the movies, and *so did I.*
>
> I like New York, and Alice likes New York.
>
> I like New York, and *so does Alice.*

Rewrite the words in italics using the correct auxiliary and so.

1. She studied English, and *I studied English.*   *so did I*

2. You will be late, and *she will be late.*

3. They have seen that movie, and *I have seen that movie.*

4. He knows her well, and *I know her well.*

5. He can swim well, and *she can swim well.*

6. He wanted to go there, and *I wanted to go there.*

7. Penny will be absent from class, and *Gloria will be absent from class.*

8. I saw the accident, and *my wife saw the accident.*

9. She has many friends, and *her husband has many friends.*

10. Tom was arrested, and *his accomplice was arrested.*

11. He arrived late, and *I arrived late.*

12. She likes to watch TV, and *her husband likes to watch TV.*

13. They enjoyed the show, and *we enjoyed the show.*

14. The meat was salty, and *the vegetables were salty.*

15. I had to get up early, and *my wife had to get up early.*

16. We'll be here tomorrow, and *Josie will be here tomorrow.*

17. He would like to see the movie, and *I would like to see the movie.*

18. Your watch is fast, and *my watch is fast.*

19. She is studying French, and *her husband is studying French.*

ABBREVIATED CLAUSES

With *Either* and *Neither* 1

We use *either* and *neither* to avoid repetition in negative sentences.

> He doesn't like jazz, and she doesn't like jazz.
>
> He doesn't like jazz, and she *doesn't either.*
>
> He doesn't like jazz, and *neither does she.*
>
> Susan didn't go to the concert, and I didn't go to the concert.
>
> Susan didn't go to the concert, and I *didn't either.*
>
> Susan didn't go to the concert, and *neither did I.*

Rewrite the words in italics using the correct auxiliary and either.

1. She didn't like the movie, and *I didn't like the movie.*   *I didn't either*

2. We won't be there, and *Louise won't be there.* _____

3. He doesn't study much, and *she doesn't study much.* _____

4. Edna isn't going to the party, and *I'm not going to the party.* _____

5. I don't like the climate there, and *my wife doesn't like the climate there.* _____

6. Debbie won't be able to go, and *I won't be able to go.* _____

7. I didn't see the accident, and *Rick didn't see the accident.* _____

8. You won't like that picture, and *your wife won't like that picture.* _____

9. I haven't seen that movie, and *Molly hasn't seen that movie.* _____

10. He didn't arrive on time, and *we didn't arrive on time.* _____

11. She doesn't have many friends, and *he doesn't have many friends.* _____

12. Angie can't go, and *I can't go.* _____

13. I'm not sorry about it, and *Grace isn't sorry about it.* _____

14. You can't blame me for that mistake, and *George can't blame me for that mistake.* _____

15. My watch doesn't run well, and *your watch doesn't run well.* _____

16. I didn't remember his name, and *Henry didn't remember his name.* _____

Rewrite the words in italics using the correct auxiliary and neither.

1. She didn't like the concert, and *I didn't like the concert.*   *neither did I*

2. He didn't hear me, and *the teacher didn't hear me.*   _____

3. I can't speak Spanish, and *my wife can't speak Spanish.*   _____

4. He hasn't read the book, and *I haven't read the book.*   _____

5. They didn't enjoy the novel, and *we didn't enjoy the novel.*   _____

6. I couldn't hear him well, and *Yoko couldn't hear him well.*   _____

7. We don't have a TV, and *they don't have a TV.*   _____

8. Cecile can't go, and *Gail can't go.*   _____

9. She hasn't said anything about it, and *I haven't said anything about it.*   _____

10. I won't be at the meeting, and *George won't be at the meeting.*   _____

11. I didn't hear anyone in the room, and *my wife didn't hear anyone in the room.*   _____

12. He hasn't prepared his homework, and *I haven't prepared my homework.*   _____

13. Your answer isn't correct, and *my answer isn't correct.*   _____

14. He doesn't eat lunch there, and *his friends don't eat lunch there.*   _____

15. Gertrude isn't going to the party, and *I'm not going to the party.*   _____

16. He didn't have any money with him, and *I didn't have any money with me.*   _____

17. Pete can't go with us, and *Rodney can't go with us.*   _____

18. You won't enjoy that show, and *your wife won't enjoy that show.*   _____

19. Ralph didn't see me, and *the teacher didn't see me.*   _____

ABBREVIATED CLAUSES

With Auxiliary Verbs

In sentences where we have two conflicting ideas, we avoid repetition of words and phrases by using *but* and an appropriate auxiliary.

> They can't speak French. We can speak French.
>
> They can't speak French, *but we can.*
>
> I like to ski. Harvey and Lisa don't like to ski.
>
> I like to ski, *but* Harvey and Lisa *don't.*

Use the correct auxiliary to complete the sentence. Use contracted forms for negative statements.

1. He won't be able to go, but I _____.   _____*will*_____

2. She will arrive on time, but we _____.   _____

3. I liked the movie, but my wife _____.   _____

4. Robin is going to the party, but I _____.   _____

5. She knows him well, but I _____.   _____

6. She doesn't know her lesson well, but I _____.   _____

7. I prepared my lesson, but she _____.   _____

8. He arrived on time, but his wife _____.   _____

9. She won't lend you any money, but I _____.   _____

10. Henry has seen that movie, but I _____.   _____

11. I have never been to Europe, but my wife _____.   _____

12. Alex can speak English, but his sons _____.   _____

13. Grace came home for lunch, but Helen _____.   _____

14. She plays the piano well, but her sister _____.   _____

15. My wife doesn't want to go to the concert, but I _____.   _____

16. She enjoys living in the north, but her husband _____.   _____

17. Murray isn't going to the beach, but I _____.   _____

18. At first, I didn't like living in New York, but now I _____.   _____

19. She says she knows him well, but I don't think she _____.   _____

20. They don't have class tomorrow, but we _____.   _____

Write the noun form that corresponds to each adjective.

1.	curious	*curiosity*	26.	ignorant	
2.	innocent	*innocence*	27.	emphatic	
3.	proud		28.	strange	
4.	sick		29.	happy	
5.	different		30.	free	
6.	simple		31.	weak	
7.	foolish		32.	ill	
8.	young		33.	sympathetic	
9.	sad		34.	dangerous	
10.	important		35.	dignified	
11.	difficult		36.	absent	
12.	angry		37.	kind	
13.	deep		38.	religious	
14.	strong		39.	true	
15.	high		40.	silent	
16.	nervous		41.	intelligent	
17.	dead		42.	generous	
18.	beautiful		43.	jealous	
19.	convenient		44.	cruel	
20.	ugly		45.	confident	
21.	gentle		46.	wealthy	
22.	bitter		47.	healthy	
23.	possible		48.	anxious	
24.	wide		49.	mysterious	
25.	sarcastic		50.	noisy	

NOUN AND ADJECTIVE FORMS 2

Write the adjective form that corresponds to each noun.

1. success _____successful_____
2. enthusiasm _____enthusiastic_____
3. advantage _____
4. sarcasm _____
5. anger _____
6. fortune _____
7. humor _____
8. dignity _____
9. mercy _____
10. patience _____
11. energy _____
12. dirt _____
13. absence _____
14. necessity _____
15. beauty _____
16. disgrace _____
17. rain _____
18. wave _____
19. affection _____
20. mystery _____
21. suspicion _____
22. style _____
23. pride _____
24. sentiment _____

25. religion _____
26. ignorance _____
27. noise _____
28. truth _____
29. ambition _____
30. power _____
31. silence _____
32. importance _____
33. depth _____
34. height _____
35. width _____
36. length _____
37. strength _____
38. cruelty _____
39. intelligence _____
40. presence _____
41. generosity _____
42. bitterness _____
43. death _____
44. freedom _____
45. simplicity _____
46. confusion _____
47. indifference _____
48. regularity _____

The perfect form of the infinitive is used to describe an action that happened before the time of the main verb of the sentence. Form the perfect form of the infinitive with *have* and the past participle of the principal verb.

> I am glad *to have met* you.
>
> We were sorry not *to have gone* to the play while it was in town.
>
> You are smart *to have bought* your winter clothes during the sale.

Write the infinitive in the perfect form. Note how the order of actions is evident.

1. I am sorry *to tell* you this.   *to have told*
2. He is thought *to be* the best person for the job.   _____
3. You are lucky *to have* so many good friends.   _____
4. I am sorry *to miss* such an important meeting.   _____
5. It is a pleasure *to work* for him.   _____
6. I am glad *to meet* you.   _____
7. I am happy *to know* you.   _____
8. It is an honor *to know* such a distinguished woman.   _____
9. You are wise *to do* that right away.   _____
10. I am glad *to see* you again.   _____
11. He is lucky *to have* you as a friend.   _____
12. She is said *to be* the strongest person in the government.   _____
13. The train is supposed *to arrive* at five o'clock.   _____
14. You ought *to do* this right away.   _____
15. You are very wise *to save* your money.   _____
16. She is lucky *to know* about this beforehand.   _____
17. I am sorry not *to be able* to talk with her.   _____
18. She seems *to like* him a lot.   _____
19. They ought *to deliver* this immediately.   _____
20. You were wrong *to show* him so little respect.   _____

MUST HAVE, MIGHT HAVE

Must have shows a strong probability that something happened in the past. It is followed by the past participle.

> By the looks of the street, it *must have rained* while we were in the movie theater.

Might have expresses a possibility that something happened in the past. It is also followed by the past participle.

> They *might have sent* an e-mail message. Let me check.

A. *Write the past perfect form of* must *in the sentence.*

1. I cannot find my book. I (leave) it at home.   *must have left*

2. You (come) here by taxi.   _____

3. He speaks English so well that he (live) in England for many years.   _____

4. Gail (leave) home during the morning because she was not there when I called at noon.   _____

5. I imagine, from things they have told me, that they (be) very wealthy at one time.   _____

6. Paula (study) very hard before her exam.   _____

7. She (be) a very smart woman when she was younger.   _____

8. You (work) fast in order to have finished so quickly.   _____

B. *Write the past perfect form of* might *in the sentence.*

1. I haven't any idea where Joy is. She (go) to the movies with Tim.   *might have gone*

2. The bad weather (delay) them.   _____

3. You (lost) your keys on the bus.   _____

4. It's strange Joe is not here for his appointment, but he (forget) all about it.   _____

5. One of the strangers (steal) the money.   _____

6. Al (take) your book by mistake.   _____

7. They (called) while we were out.   _____

8. They (be) wealthy at one time, but I doubt it.   _____

Write the correct form of the verb in parentheses in the conditional sentence.

1. If I had known about this yesterday, I (help) him.   _would have helped_

2. If I (be) you, I would not mention it to him.   _____

3. I would have gone if I (have) the time.   _____

4. If I see her, I (give) her your message.   _____

5. If he had been driving any faster, he (have) an accident.   _____

6. If I could help you, I (do) so gladly.   _____

7. If the weather were warm today, we (go) to the beach.   _____

8. If the weather had been warm yesterday, we (go) to the beach.   _____

9. If I (see) Rose, I will tell her the good news.   _____

10. If we decide to go, we (let) you know.   _____

11. I would have bought the car if I (have) the money.   _____

12. He will pass his exams if he (study) hard.   _____

13. He would pass his exams if he (study) hard.   _____

14. He would have passed his exams if he (study) hard.   _____

15. If I took the noon train, I (arrive) in Tokyo at nine.   _____

16. I would certainly have given her the message if I (see) her.   _____

17. If it were not raining, I (work) in my garden.   _____

18. If I (have) your telephone number, I would have called you.   _____

19. Joan would have gone with us if she (not be) ill.   _____

20. If Ana had been with us, the accident (not happen).   _____

21. Perhaps the man would not have died if there (be) a doctor present.   _____

22. If I were a millionaire, I (spend) all my winters in Florida.   _____

NEGATIVE FORM

Review 6

Change the sentence to the negative form.

1. She speaks English well.   _does not speak_
2. We went to the movies last night.   _____
3. She ought to tell him about it.   _____
4. He should have told her about it.   _____
5. He has lived there for many years.   _____
6. They were supposed to arrive yesterday.   _____
7. She can speak Spanish perfectly.   _____
8. She will return at five o'clock.   _____
9. He had to work late last night.   _____
10. He has three brothers.   _____
11. She is the best student in our class.   _____
12. You may park here.   _____
13. There were many students absent from class today.   _____
14. They were driving very fast at the time.   _____
15. I would like to have that kind of job.   _____
16. They go to the beach on Sunday.   _____
17. She knows him well.   _____
18. They got married in June.   _____
19. We should lend him more money.   _____
20. We arrived at the theater on time.   _____
21. She listens to her mother.   _____
22. They will go without us.   _____
23. He eats a lot.   _____
24. He has been studying English a long time.   _____
25. We waited a long time.   _____
26. They had left the house when I called.   _____
27. I liked the movie, and so did he.   _____

Select the correct form. Write your answer in the blank.

1. To *look up* something is to (search for it, watch it, find information about it, admire it).

   <u>find information about it</u>

2. If someone *finds out* something, she (shows it to someone, invents it, learns information about it, gives it to someone).

   _____

3. When someone says *I get it*, it means (I understand it, I bring it, I like it, I enter it).

   _____

4. To *call off* means to (make a phone call, cancel, invite people, shout).

   _____

5. To *get off* a bus means to (exit, ride, board, refuse) it.

   _____

6. If I say that I will be back *by* 8:00, this means that I will be back (exactly at 8:00, about 8:00, at 8:00 at the latest).

   _____

7. If I say that I will do it *as soon as* I get home, this means I will do it (immediately after, before, a while after) I get home.

   _____

8. To *get over* something means to (end, return to, need, recover from) it.

   _____

9. If you *give up* doing something, you (stop trying, remember to do it, share it, make plans to do it).

   _____

10. *I'd rather* go means that I (want to, prefer to, have to, seldom) go.

    _____

11. To *call back* means to (ask for help, borrow money, return a phone call, say again).

    _____

12. *Pretty good* means (very good, more or less good, extremely good, not at all good).

    _____

13. *Once in a while* means (sometimes, for a long time, only one time, forever).

    _____

14. If I *pick out* something, I (erase, lift, choose, remove) it. _____

15. To *put off* means to (remove, extinguish, uncover, postpone). _____

16. If you *think over* something, you (forget, remember, consider, dream about) it.

    _____

17. *Lately* means (often, very soon, recently, later). _____

Proper and Common Nouns

Nouns refer to people, places, things, or ideas. Nouns that are the names of specific people, places, or things are called *proper nouns*. Proper nouns are always capitalized.

Types of proper nouns	Examples of proper nouns
Names of people, including their titles	*George, Ms. Jones, Dr. Einstein*
Names of months, holidays, and days of the week	*December, Independence Day, Tuesday*
Names of places and geographical features	*New York City, Thailand, Maple Street, Andes Mountains*
Names of buildings and monuments	*Empire State Building, Eiffel Tower*
Names of businesses and institutions	*Microsoft Corporation, London School of Economics, United Nations*
Names of languages and nationalities	*Chinese, French, Mexican, Brazilian*
Names of religions	*Buddhism, Christianity, Islam*
Titles of courses*	*Intermediate English, Introduction to Biology*
Titles of movies, TV programs, and publications*	*The Matrix, Grammar to Go, Newsweek*

*In titles, don't capitalize a small word, such as *of* or *the*, unless it is the first word of the title.

Don't confuse common nouns with proper nouns. Proper nouns are specific names; common nouns are not specific names, but are more general terms.

Proper nouns	Common nouns
This car belongs to *Dr. Johnson*.	You should visit the *doctor* when you are sick.
The *Mississippi River* is very long.	I like to go swimming in the *river*.
We plan to visit the *Washington Monument*.	It is a famous *monument*.
I graduated from *Central High School*.	It is a very big *school*.
Sarah is taking *Advanced Mathematics* this semester.	She is very interested in *mathematics*.

Noncount nouns are nouns that don't have a plural form. Often they are things that cannot be counted.

Examples of common noncount nouns

Food	Liquids and gases	Materials
meat	water	metal
flour	milk	gold
sugar	coffee	silver
butter	shampoo	wood
cereal	oil	cotton
fruit	ink	silk
bread	paint	nylon
beef	air	plastic
salt	oxygen	plaster
pepper	steam	clay
soup	smog	glass

Groups of things	Abstract ideas	Weather
furniture	information	rain
luggage	advice	thunder
jewelry	love	lightning
equipment	beauty	cold
mail	education	heat
money	knowledge	snow
traffic	sadness	ice
vocabulary	anger	fog
	intelligence	wind

Pronouns

Pronouns take the place of nouns.

Subject pronouns are used in the subject position in a sentence.

Sam and Sarah are our neighbors. *They* live next door.

	Singular	Plural
1st person	I	we
2nd person	you	you
3rd person	he, she, it	they

Object pronouns are used in the object position (following a verb or preposition) in a sentence.

Do you like my new shoes? I bought *them* yesterday.

	Singular	Plural
1st person	me	us
2nd person	you	you
3rd person	him, her, it	them

Possessive pronouns take the place of possessive nouns or possessive adjectives plus nouns.

That isn't my coat. *Mine* is in the closet.

	Singular	Plural
1st person	mine	ours
2nd person	yours	yours
3rd person	his, hers, its	theirs

Reflexive pronouns are used when the subject and the object of a sentence refer to the same person or thing.

> John cut *himself*.

They are used with the preposition *by* to mean *alone* or *without help*.

> Sharon wrote the composition by *herself*.

They are used to emphasize a noun.

> Teachers *themselves* sometimes make mistakes.

	Singular	Plural
1st person	myself	ourselves
2nd person	yourself	yourselves
3rd person	himself herself itself	themselves

Spelling Rules for Adding Endings to Words

Adding *s* to nouns to form the plural

most nouns: add *s*	book	books
	pencil	pencils
nouns that end in *s, sh, ch, x, z*: add *es*	dress	dresses
	wish	wishes
	match	matches
	fox	foxes
	buzz	buzzes
nouns that end in a consonant plus *y*: change the *y* to *i* and add *es*	baby	babies
	city	cities
nouns that end in a vowel plus *y*: add *s* only	boy	boys
	day	days
nouns that end in *f* or *fe*: change the *f* or *fe* to *ve* and add *s*. (exceptions: belief-beliefs, roof-roofs, chief-chiefs)	leaf	leaves
	wolf	wolves
	life	lives
some nouns that end in a consonant plus *o*: add *es*	tomato	tomatoes
	hero	heroes
nouns that end in a vowel plus *o*: add *s* only	studio	studios

Adding *s* to present tense verbs to form the third-person singular

most verbs: add *s*	walk	walks
	clean	cleans
verbs that end in *s, sh, ch, x, z*: add *es*	pass	passes
	rush	rushes
	catch	catches
	fix	fixes
	fizz	fizzes
verbs that end in a consonant plus *y*: change the *y* to *i* and add *es*	carry	carries
	study	studies
verbs that end in a vowel plus *y*: add *s* only	stay	stays
	buy	buys
(irregular forms: do-does, go-goes, have-has)		

Adding *ing* to verbs for continuous tenses

most verbs: add *ing*	walk clean	walking cleaning
verbs that end in silent *e*: drop the *e* and add *ing*	write dance	writing dancing
verbs that end in a consonant-vowel-consonant pattern in a stressed syllable: double the final consonant before adding *ing*	plan stop begin	planning stopping beginning
verbs that end in a consonant-vowel-consonant pattern in an unstressed syllable: add *ing* only	listen visit	listening visiting
verbs that end in *ie*: change the *ie* to *y* and add *ing*	tie lie	tying lying

Adding *ed* to regular verbs to form the past tense

most verbs: add *ed*	walk clean	walked cleaned
verbs that end in *e*: add *d* only	hope live	hoped lived
verbs that end in a consonant-vowel-consonant pattern in a stressed syllable: double the final consonant before adding *ed*	plan stop permit	planned stopped permitted
verbs that end in a consonant-vowel-consonant pattern in an unstressed syllable: add *ed* only	listen visit	listened visited
verbs that end in a consonant plus *y*: change the *y* to *i* and add *ed*	carry study	carried studied
verbs that end in a vowel plus *y*: add *ed* only	stay enjoy	stayed enjoyed

Adding *er* and *est* to adjectives to form comparatives and superlatives

most one-syllable adjectives: add *er* for the comparative and *est* for the superlative	tall old	taller older	the tallest the oldest
adjectives that end in *e*: add *r* or *st*	safe nice	safer nicer	the safest the nicest
adjectives that end in a consonant-vowel-consonant pattern: double the final consonant and add *er* or *est*	fat hot	fatter hotter	the fattest the hottest
adjectives that end in a consonant plus *y*: change the *y* to *i* and add *er* or *est*	funny easy	funnier easier	the funniest the easiest

Irregular comparative and superlative forms

Adjective	Comparative	Superlative
good	better	the best
bad	worse	the worst
far	farther	the farthest

To Be

	Simple Present	Present Continuous	Simple Past	Present Perfect	Past Perfect
I	am	am being	was	have been	had been
you, we, they	are	are being	were	have been	had been
he, she, it	is	is being	was	has been	had been

Present Tenses

	Simple Present	Present Continuous	Present Perfect	Present Perfect Continuous
I	work	am working	have worked	have been working
you, we, they	work	are working	have worked	have been working
he, she, it	works	is working	has worked	has been working

Past Tenses

	Simple Past	Past Continuous	Past Perfect	Past Perfect Continuous
I	worked	was working	had worked	had been working
you, we, they	worked	were working	had worked	had been working
he, she, it	worked	was working	had worked	had been working

Future Tenses

	Simple Future	Future Continuous	Future Perfect
I	will work	will be working	will have worked
you, we, they	will work	will be working	will have worked
he, she, it	will work	will be working	will have worked

Passive Voice

The passive voice is formed with the verb *to be* and the past participle form of the verb. The passive voice can be used in all verb tenses.

Tense	Active Voice	Passive Voice
Simple Present	Sam answers the phone.	The phone is answered by Sam.
Present Continuous	Sam is answering the phone.	The phone is being answered by Sam.
Present Perfect	Sam has answered the phone.	The phone has been answered by Sam.
Simple Past	Sam answered the phone.	The phone was answered by Sam.
Past Continuous	Sam was answering the phone.	The phone was being answered by Sam.
Past Perfect	Sam had answered the phone.	The phone had been answered by Sam.
Simple Future	Sam will answer the phone.	The phone will be answered by Sam.

Conditional Sentences

A conditional sentence consists of an *if* clause and a result clause.

- **Future real** conditional sentences use the present tense in the *if* clause and the future tense in the result clause. The modals *can, may*, and *might* are also possible in the result clause.

- **Present unreal** conditionals use the past tense in the *if* clause and *would* plus verb in the result clause. The modals *could* and *might* are also possible in the result clause. The correct form of the verb *to be* in the *if* clause is always *were*.

- **Past unreal** conditionals use the past perfect form of the verb in the *if* clause and *would have* plus the past participle in the result clause. *Could have* and *might have* are also possible in the result clause.

	If Clause	Result Clause
Future Real	If you *stay* up late tonight,	you *will be* very tired tomorrow.
	If we *have* enough time,	we *may go* to the movies on Friday.
Present Unreal	If you *stayed* up late every night,	you *would be* very tired.
	If we *had* more free time,	we *could go* out more often.
	If I *were* at the beach right now,	I *would swim* all day.
Past Unreal	If you *had stayed* up late last night,	you *would have been* very tired.
	If we *had had* more time last weekend,	we *might have gone* to the movies.

APPENDIX: GRAMMAR SUMMARY

Common Irregular Verbs

Many common verbs are irregular in their past and past participle forms.

PRESENT	PAST	PAST PARTICIPLE	PRESENT	PAST	PAST PARTICIPLE
become	became	become	hang	hung	hung
begun	began	begun	have	had	had
bet	bet	bet	hear	heard	heard
bite	bit	bitten	hide	hid	hidden
begin	began	begun	hit	hit	hit
blow	blew	blown	hold	held	held
break	broke	broken	hurt	hurt	hurt
bring	brought	brought			
build	built	built	keep	kept	kept
burst	burst	burst	kneel	knelt	knelt
buy	bought	bought	know	knew	known
catch	caught	caught	lead	led	led
choose	chose	chosen	leave	left	left
come	came	come	lend	lent	lent
cost	cost	cost	let	let	let
creep	crept	crept	lie	lay	lain
cut	cut	cut	lose	lost	lost
deal	dealt	dealt	make	made	made
dig	dug	dug	mean	meant	meant
do	did	done	meet	met	met
draw	drew	drawn			
drink	drank	drunk	pay	paid	paid
drive	drove	driven	put	put	put
eat	ate	eaten	read	read	read
			ride	rode	ridden
fall	fell	fallen	ring	rang	rung
feed	fed	fed	run	ran	run
feel	felt	felt			
fight	fought	fought	say	said	said
find	found	found	see	saw	seen
fly	flew	flown	sell	sold	sold
forget	forgot	forgotten	send	sent	sent
freeze	froze	frozen	set	set	set
			shake	shook	shaken
get	got	gotten	shine	shone	shone
give	gave	given	shoot	shot	shot
go	went	gone	shrink	shrank	shrunk
grow	grew	grown	shut	shut	shut

PRESENT	PAST	PAST PARTICIPLE
sing	sang	sung
sink	sank	sunk
sit	sat	sat
sleep	slept	slept
speak	spoke	spoken
spend	spent	spent
spin	spun	spun
split	split	split
spread	spread	spread
spring	sprang	sprung
stand	stood	stood
steal	stole	stolen
sweep	swept	swept
swim	swam	swum

PRESENT	PAST	PAST PARTICIPLE
take	took	taken
teach	taught	taught
tear	tore	torn
tell	told	told
think	thought	thought
throw	threw	thrown
understand	understood	understood
wear	wore	worn
win	won	won
write	wrote	written

Page 1

2. his 3. our 4. their 5. her 6. its 7. Her
8. your 9. my 10. her 11. our 12. his
13. my 14. their 15. their 16. her 17. its
18. your 19. her 20. his 21. his

Page 2

2. us 3. them 4. them 5. you 6. it 7. them
8. it 9. them 10. it 11. her 12. it 13. them
14. it 15. them 16. him/her 17. us 18. her
19. him

Page 3

2. myself 3. himself 4. ourselves 5. themselves
6. myself 7. itself 8. herself 9. ourselves
10. themselves 11. himself/herself 12. myself
13. himself 14. himself

Page 4

2. theirs 3. mine 4. his 5. ours 6. his
7. yours 8. yours 9. hers 10. mine 11. theirs
12. ours 13. mine 14. yours 15. yours
16. hers 17. his 18. yours 19. theirs 20. hers

Page 5

2. ties 3. classes 4. teachers 5. beaches
6. windows 7. doors 8. dresses 9. watches
10. books 11. oxen 12. pencils 13. cafeterias
14. students 15. wishes 16. headaches 17. boxes
18. schools 19. children 20. notebooks
21. hands 22. mice 23. hats 24. geese
25. losses 26. people 27. covers 28. buses
29. feet 30. dishes 31. men 32. kisses
33. faces 34. churches 35. cousins 36. pens

Page 6

2. rugs 3. teeth 4. cities 5. tables 6. knives
7. foxes 8. potatoes 9. passes 10. boys
11. streets 12. exercises 13. echoes 14. copies
15. wolves 16. keys 17. sandwiches 18. heroes
19. trays 20. armies 21. halves 22. thieves
23. leaves 24. addresses 25. curtains 26. latches
27. letters 28. hats 29. butterflies 30. days
31. feet 32. ladies 33. babies 34. wives

Page 7

2. likes 3. plays 4. goes 5. carries 6. teaches
7. shows 8. does 9. watches 10. tries
11. speaks 12. notices 13. says 14. passes
15. washes 16. catches 17. brings 18. leaves
19. knows 20. thinks 21. sees 22. laughs
23. matches 24. dances 25. replies 26. pays
27. sings 28. fixes 29. pushes 30. pulls
31. dresses 32. misses

Page 8

3. She must go 4. She fixes 5. She has 6. She
will see 7. She may study 8. She lives 9. She
studies 10. She will be 11. She can go 12. She
should study 13. She plays 14. She carries
15. She goes 16. She should go 17. She can wait
18. She waits 19. She enjoys 20. She will enjoy
21. She watches 22. She likes 23. She must see
24. She passes 25. She will take 26. She teaches
27. She may work 28. She works 29. She wants
30. She does 31. She wishes 32. She can meet
33. She tries 34. She leaves 35. She uses 36. She
washes 37. She sings 38. She will know 39. She
must try 40. She replies 41. She will try 42. She
should see 43. She must have 44. She will fix

Page 9

2. has 3. study 4. studies 5. work 6. come
7. explain 8. teaches 9. watch 10. listens
11. play 12. live 13. lives 14. goes 15. come
16. does 17. makes 18. speak 19. want
20. have 21. has 22. plays 23. goes 24. stays
25. spin 26. begins

Page 10

2. These are 3. We are 4. They like 5. Those
books belong 6. They were 7. The boys do
8. They are writing 9. The children are 10. These
pencils belong 11. The tomatoes are 12. The dishes
are 13. The classes have started. 14. The women
are waiting. 15. These books are 16. We are going
to study 17. They are making 18. The buses are
19. The men have left. 20. They will leave 21. They
can speak 22. The boys must study 23. They were
24. The leaves are falling 25. The wives of Henry VIII
were not 26. The people have gone

Page 11

2. low 3. depart 4. outside 5. tame 6. asleep
7. cowardly 8. soft 9. dull 10. rough 11. lend
12. backward 13. rude 14. thin 15. after
16. behind 17. cheap 18. wet 19. true
20. parent 21. full 22. pull 23. narrow
24. tight 25. dirty 26. present 27. ugly
28. sad 29. difficult 30. wide 31. find/win
32. high 33. over 34. west 35. south 36. early
37. sell 38. short 39. seldom 40. sour
41. effect 42. bad 43. winter 44. little/small
45. lose 46. forget 47. past 48. worst

Page 12

2. with 3. in 4. by 5. to 6. to 7. from
8. for 9. in 10. around 11. in 12. at
13. for 14. in 15. for 16. by 17. at
18. about 19. for 20. on 21. to 22. to
23. for 24. by

PAGE 13

2. is running   3. have lived   4. were   5. me
6. are having   7. much   8. me   9. anyone
10. has worked   11. comes   12. on   13. get
14. wrote   15. us   16. want   17. to learn
18. live   19. These   20. an   21. has   22. are
there   23. themselves   24. His

PAGE 14

2. forced   3. studied   4. indicated   5. needed
6. learned   7. practiced   8. used   9. married
10. managed   11. carried   12. played
13. guided   14. stopped   15. hoped   16. cried
17. seemed   18. enjoyed   19. appeared
20. noticed   21. traveled   22. pleased   23. spelled
24. faced   25. worried   26. depended
27. decreased   28. hopped   29. pointed
30. supposed   31. referred   32. insisted

PAGE 15

3. 2   4. 1   5. 2   6. 1   7. 1   8. 1   9. 2   10. 1
11. 2   12. 1   13. 1   14. 1   15. 2   16. 1
17. 1   18. 2   19. 1   20. 1   21. 1   22. 2
23. 1   24. 2   25. 1   26. 1   27. 2   28. 1
29. 1   30. 2   31. 1   32. 1   33. 2   34. 1
35. 1   36. 1   37. 2   38. 1   39. 1   40. 1

PAGE 16

2. bought   3. lost   4. left   5. meant   6. caught
7. brought   8. swept   9. dealt   10. taught
11. thought   12. felt   13. crept   14. kept
15. knelt   16. left   17. meant   18. kept
19. bought

PAGE 17

2. found   3. met   4. held   5. sat   6. struck
7. read   8. found   9. led   10. hung   11. fought
12. held   13. dug   14. shone   15. fed

PAGE 18

3. isn't   4. isn't   5. weren't   6. isn't studying
7. isn't talking   8. aren't   9. isn't   10. aren't
going   11. aren't   12. isn't   13. wasn't
14. weren't   15. weren't   16. am not/'m not
17. isn't   18. weren't   19. aren't going
20. aren't working   21. isn't standing

PAGE 19

2. mustn't   3. may not   4. might not   5. can't
6. may not   7. shouldn't   8. won't   9. can't
10. might not   11. can't   12. can't   13. won't
14. won't   15. might not   16. may not
17. might not   18. won't   19. can't   20. mustn't
21. may not

PAGE 20

2. don't live   3. don't know   4. didn't eat   5. don't
want   6. didn't stop   7. didn't cook   8. didn't sit
9. doesn't read   10. doesn't speak   11. doesn't eat
12. didn't come   13. didn't have   14. didn't drink
15. didn't watch   16. didn't hang   17. didn't find
18. don't sit   19. didn't learn   20. didn't hold

PAGE 21

2. doesn't speak   3. isn't raining   4. isn't
5. weren't   6. didn't meet   7. didn't win
8. won't be   9. didn't come   10. doesn't feel
11. wasn't   12. aren't going   13. can't speak
14. shouldn't park   15. shouldn't spend   16. don't
go   17. don't like   18. isn't   19. won't tell
20. didn't call   21. isn't wearing   22. didn't leave
23. don't understand   24. doesn't speak   25. wasn't
sleeping   26. didn't go   27. hasn't seen

PAGE 22

2. Is he   3. Is she   4. Was George   5. Were they
tired   6. Is she   7. Is Lily   8. Are Mr. and Mrs.
Kim   9. Are they angry?   10. Is she studying
11. Is Anil playing   12. Are they making   13. Is he
14. Were there   15. Was he hungry   16. Were they
17. Were they   18. Is it raining   19. Are they
going   20. Were you   21. Is there   22. Were we
23. Were they arguing

PAGE 23

2. Can she speak   3. Should she study   4. May he sit
5. Will they be   6. Can she run   7. Can he go
8. Should he mention   9. Will they be   10. Should
she study   11. Will Mr. Darbari go   12. Will she call
13. Should he drink   14. Can we use   15. Should he
study   16. Will they become   17. May we leave
18. Will it rain   19. May we sit   20. Will she be
21. Should our friends   22. Must this file   23. Can
she go

PAGE 24

2. Did they leave   3. Does she study   4. Did he buy
5. Does she drive   6. Did Daniela answer   7. Did he
sit   8. Does he speak   9. Do they go   10. Did they
meet   11. Did Billy cut   12. Did she give   13. Do
they live   14. Do you drink   15. Does the bus come
16. Did the train arrive   17. Does he write   18. Did
they bring   19. Did he lose   20. Did they catch

PAGE 25

2. When will he be here?   3. Why are they tired?
4. How many hours does he work?   5. How long did
they spend in the park?   6. Where does she live?
7. When can she have dinner at our house?   8. What
time did it ring?   9. Why is he walking fast?
10. How much coffee do you need?   11. When will

she tell us? 12. What time did it leave? 13. How long did it rain? 14. What time will it arrive? 15. Where should I hang it up? 16. Why is he/she crying? 17. What did they forget? 18. Where did he invite them? 19. How many children do they have? 20. When can she visit?

PAGE 26

3. (blank) 4. the 5. (blank) 6. The
7. (blank) 8. The 9. (blank) 10. (blank)
11. (blank) 12. The

PAGE 27

2. is ringing 3. writes 4. is writing 5. reads
6. reads 7. is read 8. rains 9. is beginning
10. is knocking 11. stops 12. is stopping 13. get
14. are building 15. have 16. are having 17. is
waving 18. comes 19. is sleeping 20. sleeps

PAGE 28

2. were sitting 3. was shining 4. was walking
5. were having 6. was studying 7. was playing
8. were driving 9. was writing 10. was getting
11. was preparing 12. was raining 13. was shining
14. was talking 15. were watching 16. was
cooking 17. were sleeping 18. was suffering

PAGE 29

2. was sleeping 3. was blowing 4. rained 5. was
raining 6. was playing 7. played 8. were having
9. read 10. was reading 11. wrote 12. was
writing 13. was shining 14. rang 15. drove
16. was driving 17. played 18. was playing
19. saw 20. was leaving 21. waited 22. were
waiting 23. painted 24. was painting 25. went
26. was going

PAGE 30

2. on 3. at 4. from 5. to 6. at 7. with
8. by 9. over 10. on 11. to/with 12. with
13. on 14. in 15. for 16. in 17. at 18. for
19. for 20. for 21. about 22. of 23. with
24. about 25. from

PAGE 31

2. do 3. were 4. an 5. an 6. These 7. mine
8. were 9. eat 10. is playing 11. for 12. saw
13. were eating 14. comes 15. her 16. is riding
17. was raining 18. has worked 19. has 20. buy
21. were 22. studies 23. are taking 24. were
25. are

PAGE 32

2. has to go 3. has to leave 4. have to be
5. have to learn 6. have to have 7. has to work

8. has to go 9. have to wait 10. have to go
11. has to spend 12. have to go 13. has to be
14. have to leave 15. have to write 16. has to
write 17. have to remain 18. have to get 19. has
to stay 20. has to visit 21. have to meet 22. have
to finish 23. has to watch

PAGE 33

A. 2. had to leave 3. had to work 4. had to get
up 5. had to walk 6. had to have

B. 2. will have to return 3. will have to do
4. will have to be 5. will have to buy 6. will
have to wait

C. 2. has had to learn 3. have had to go
4. have had to return 5. have had to call
6. has had to cook 7. have had to study

PAGE 34

2. didn't have to leave 3. don't have to study
4. don't have to write 5. didn't have to wait
6. doesn't have to spend 7. don't have to return
8. doesn't have to be 9. don't have to leave
10. didn't have to walk 11. won't have to send
12. don't have to wait 13. didn't have to pay
14. didn't have to go 15. don't have to cash
16. won't have to invite 17. doesn't have to take
18. didn't have to join 19. doesn't have to leave
20. don't have to write 21. didn't have to write

PAGE 35

2. Did he have to stay 3. Do the students have to
learn 4. Will they have to write 5. Did she have to
wait 6. Do you have to return 7. Did she have to
go 8. Does she have to take 9. Did we have to
invite 10. Does he have to leave 11. Will we have
to write 12. Do they have to arrive 13. Does Tom
have to get up 14. Does Sue have to help 15. Did
she have to prepare 16. Does she have to work
17. Did they have to stay 18. Does he have to go
19. Do I have to sign 20. Did we have to send

PAGE 36

2. said 3. said 4. tells 5. told 6. said
7. said 8. told 9. said 10. said 11. told
12. told 13. tell

PAGE 37

2. lived 3. began 4. has studied 5. studied
6. began 7. were 8. have lived 9. worked
10. have worked 11. have been 12. became
13. has been

PAGE 38

2. one pound 3. one mile 4. seven ante meridian
5. six post meridian 6. five tenths 7. one half

8. one fourth/quarter   9. six percent   10. number
five   11. sixty-eight degrees   12. alternating current
13. direct current   14. et cetera   15. one gallon
16. television   17. quart   18. pint   19. yard
20. inch   21. and   22. Incorporated   23. two years
24. four feet   25. Ninety-sixth Street   26. Avenue
27. Boulevard   28. Road   29. Building
30. February   31. August   32. December
33. square foot/feet   34. first   35. third
36. seventh   37. Thursday   38. Wednesday
39. New York   40. California   41. The United
States of America   42. The United Kingdom   43. at
44. one centimeter   45. five dollars   46. Eight
kilometers   47. compact disc   48. post office box

PAGE 39

2. have been living   3. have been trying   4. has
been driving   5. has been feeling   6. has been sitting
7. has been working   8. have been talking   9. has
been speaking   10. has been working   11. have been
listening   12. have been waiting   13. has been
raining   14. have been whistling   15. has been
studying   16. has been wearing   17. have been
working   18. have been planning

PAGE 40

2. hasn't been feeling   3. haven't been discussing
4. hasn't been following   5. haven't been dating
6. hasn't been speaking   7. haven't been staying
8. hasn't been snowing   9. hasn't been studying
10. haven't been planning   11. haven't been sitting
12. hasn't been working   13. hasn't been teaching
14. haven't been waiting   15. haven't been listening

PAGE 41

2. How long has he been feeling sick?   3. How long
have they been discussing it?   4. Why has it been
following him?   5. Where have you been living?
6. What has she been reading?   7. How long have
they been staying there?   8. How long has it been
snowing?   9. What have you been thinking about?
10. How long have you been planning it?   11. Why
have they been sitting there?   12. How long has she
been working here?

PAGE 42

2. since   3. for   4. ago   5. for   6. for
7. since   8. since   9. for   10. since   11. ago
12. since   13. for   14. since   15. ago
16. since   17. for   18. since   19. ago

PAGE 43

2. had stolen   3. had taken   4. had had   5. had
found   6. had seen   7. had left   8. had played
9. had left   10. had lived 11. had looked   12. had
taken   13. had had   14. had received   15. had done

PAGE 44

2. hadn't studied   3. hadn't had   4. hadn't eaten
5. hadn't bought   6. hadn't met   7. hadn't finished
8. hadn't seen   9. hadn't left   10. hadn't lived
11. hadn't arrived   12. hadn't done   13. hadn't
worked   14. hadn't finished   15. hadn't arrived
16. hadn't washed   17. hadn't fallen   18. hadn't
begun

PAGE 45

2. had Lily and Joe known   3. had Lee studied
4. had you lived   5. had he worked   6. had Sylvia
written   7. had you worked   8. had Otto worked
9. had you walked   10. had Isabel entered
11. had Michael studied   12. had you seen
13. had we waited   14. had Ms. Kim taught
15. had she had   16. had they held

PAGE 46

2. didn't leave   3. isn't   4. didn't want   5. hasn't
studied   6. didn't tell   7. won't return   8. isn't
having   9. haven't left   10. can't speak   11. mustn't
tell   12. aren't going   13. isn't   14. wasn't
15. hasn't worked   16. haven't been living
17. doesn't have to work   18. didn't have to go
19. didn't come   20. aren't making   21. didn't tell
22. doesn't prepare   23. weren't playing   24. hasn't
finished   25. isn't   26. hadn't finished
27. hadn't had

PAGE 47

2. Did he give   3. Is she   4. Are we going
5. Will they return   6. Did he leave   7. Can
Marcia swim   8. Is she going to study   9. Has he
read   10. Has she been studying   11. Is she
12. Do we have to have   13. Did Robert have to
leave   14. Will he return   15. Were they having
16. Did they build   17. Will they deliver
18. Was she   19. Is it   20. Is the wind blowing
21. Were there   22. Did the child cut
23. Did the boy run   24. Is the doorbell ringing

PAGE 48

2. of   3. about   4. up   5. at/on   6. about
7. on   8. at/about   9. about   10. for   11. in
12. over/above   13. below   14. in   15. on
16. out   17. with   18. in   19. from   20. in
21. in   22. from   23. on   24. to

PAGE 49

2. had   3. was reading   4. yours   5. had to
6. don't have to   7. were   8. was cooking
9. bought   10. leave   11. is coming   12. are
having   13. to us   14. me to go   15. me
16. blows   17. anyone   18. went   19. have been
20. said   21. are singing   22. an   23. hadn't had

PAGE 50

2. You're 3. She's 4. It's 5. She's 6. We're
7. They're 8. There's 9. You're 10. I'll
11. You'll 12. She'll 13. We'll 14. don't
15. doesn't 16. didn't 17. won't 18. aren't
19. haven't

PAGE 51

2. for 3. for 4. to 5. for 6. for 7. to
8. to 9. for 10. to 11. to 12. for 13. to
14. to 15. to 16. to 17. to 18. to

PAGE 52

2. gave Antonia 3. sent him 4. show Rudy
5. paid the landlord 6. sold his friend 7. took her
8. brought me 9. bought his wife 10. brought us
11. send them 12. gave her father 13. sent Ms.
Pappas 14. told Sharon 15. gave each of us
16. lent his brother 17. hand me 18. sent each of
them 19. send us 20. lent us 21. bring me

PAGE 53

2. flown 3. driven 4. broke 5. broken
6. fell 7. fallen 8. did 9. drew 10. ate
11. froze 12. gave 13. chose 14. bitten
15. done

PAGE 54

2. is going to teach 3. are going to be 4. is going
to meet 5. are going to stay 6. is going to go
7. is going to take 8. are going to go 9. is going
to rain 10. are going to eat 11. is going to have
12. are going to go 13. is going to get married
14. are going to spend 15. is going to ask
16. are going to be 17. are going to go 18. are
going to fly

PAGE 55

2. was going to go 3. was going to study
4. were going to go 5. was going to see
6. were going to buy 7. were going to visit
8. was going to be 9. were going to eat
10. was going to send 11. was going to lend

PAGE 56

2. was 3. could 4. would 5. was 6. lived
7. was 8. liked 9. lived 10. could 11. would
12. might 13. was 14. had lost 15. meant
16. was 17. would 18. might 19. was

PAGE 57

3. s 4. s 5. z 6. z 7. s 8. z 9. z 10. s
11. z 12. s 13. z 14. z 15. s 16. z
17. z 18. s 19. z 20. z 21. s 22. z

23. s 24. z 25. z 26. s 27. z 28. z
29. s 30. s 31. z 32. z 33. z 34. s
35. s 36. z 37. s 38. z 39. s 40. z
41. z 42. z 43. s 44. z

PAGE 58

3. t 4. t 5. d 6. t 7. t 8. d 9. t
10. t 11. d 12. t 13. d 14. t 15. d
16. t 17. d 18. d 19. t 20. d 21. d
22. d 23. t 24. d 25. d 26. t 27. d
28. d 29. t 30. t 31. d 32. d 33. t
34. d 35. t 36. d 37. t 38. t 39. d 40. t
41. d 42. d

PAGE 59

2. get home 3. got in 4. get ready 5. gets
6. gets on 7. gets off 8. get very tired 9. got
excited 10. get over 11. got into 12. get to
13. get home 14. get sleepy 15. get married

PAGE 60

3. d 4. t 5. s 6. b 7. k 8. w, t 9. h
10. t 11. k 12. g 13. b 14. t 15. l
16. l 17. l 18. k 19. k 20. d 21. p
22. b 23. l 24. s 25. w 26. w 27. t
28. t 29. n 30. c 31. b 32. g 33. b
34. w 35. w 36. t 37. w 38. b 39. k
40. k 41. c 42. l 43. h 44. h, t 45. c
46. l 47. d 48. h 49. c 50. b

PAGE 61

2. in 3. from 4. of 5. in 6. after 7. at
8. from 9. in 10. on 11. off 12. over
13. of 14. of 15. by 16. out 17. of 18. on
19. about 20. on 21. in 22. by 23. by
24. about

PAGE 62

2. had had 3. has saved 4. were walking 5. went
6. eaten 7. me 8. me to wait 9. said 10. was
11. would 12. between 13. sits 14. is beginning
15. was 16. to 17. a lot of 18. hers 19. mine
20. told 21. could 22. were having 23. closed
24. made 25. had to have 26. hadn't, was

PAGE 63

2. Many newspaper articles are written by her.
3. The room is cleaned by the maid every day.
4. Their quarrels are heard by everyone. 5. The
mail is delivered by the letter carrier. 6. All the
letters are written by the secretary. 7. Her speeches
are enjoyed by everyone. 8. The magazine is sold by
them everywhere. 9. Our exercises are corrected by
her at home. 10. Dinner is prepared by Joe every
night. 11. The mail is delivered by them at ten

o'clock.   12. Urgent information is brought by a messenger.   13. The documents are signed by them in the courthouse.   14. Presents are brought by her from Hong Kong.   15. Our compositions are corrected by the teacher.   16. The books are printed by them in Boston.   17. The grass is cut by him once a week.   18. The papers are sent by them by express mail.   19. The contracts are prepared by the lawyer.

Page 64

2. The money was taken by someone.   3. The mail had been delivered by the letter carrier.   4. The letters have been signed by him.   5. Many books have been written by her.   6. The bills were paid by Marianne by check.   7. The work will be finished by them tomorrow.   8. The work had been finished by him in time.   9. The party has been planned by them.   10. Corn was grown by Native Americans in Mexico.   11. Several buildings have been designed by him.   12. The contract had been signed by him previously.   13. The plate was broken by her in anger.   14. The accident was seen by Julia on her way home.   15. The tickets had been bought by them.   16. The child has been found by them at last.   17. The trees will be planted by Sonia.   18. The dinner was prepared by them.   19. It will be sent by her immediately.   20. The key was used by him to open the door.

Page 65

2. It may be kept by the museum for two weeks.
3. The bill can be paid later.   4. It has to be delivered tomorrow.   5. Those things can't be put there.   6. It must be sent at once.   7. It should be delivered today.
8. It ought to be written now.   9. This work must be completed by all the students.   10. It may be brought later.   11. This room can be used by Linda.   12. It has to be done soon.

Page 66

2. will not be delivered   3. must not be signed
4. was not shot   5. is not taught   6. was not wrapped   7. was not struck   8. has not been delivered   9. was not followed   10. were not heard
11. cannot be used   12. was not printed   13. were not sent   14. will not be delivered   15. cannot be sent   16. was not taken   17. were not disappointed
18. will not be written   19. had not been decorated

Page 67

2. Was the thief captured   3. Will the lecture be attended   4. Has the dinner been served   5. Are we invited   6. Will the work be done   7. Was the city destroyed   8. Must these letters be signed   9. Was America discovered   10. Has the house been struck
11. Will his book be published   12. Should this project be finished   13. Is the mail delivered

14. Are the poems written   15. Was the car destroyed
16. Will their engagement be announced   17. Will they be married   18. Was the meeting held   19. Was it attended   20. Can all these books be borrowed

Page 68

2. (blank)   3. a   4. (blank)   5. (blank)   6. The
7. (blank)   8. The   9. the   10. an   11. (blank)
12. The   13. (blank)   14. The   15. The   16. The
17. a   18. (blank)   19. a   20. a   21. (blank)
22. The   23. the   24. (blank)   25. The

Page 69

2. torn   3. lain   4. known   5. shook   6. spoke
7. grown   8. threw   9. hid   10. worn   11. wrote
12. took   13. ridden   14. grew   15. seen
16. tore   17. spoken   18. knew   19. known

Page 70

2. weak   3. no one   4. dead   5. true   6. rude
7. careless   8. start/begin/go   9. forget   10. right
11. late   12. always   13. fast   14. cause
15. rough   16. tighten   17. retail   18. cowardly
19. buy   20. noisy/loud   21. wet   22. loose
23. backward   24. simple   25. full   26. sour
27. short   28. useful   29. decrease   30. lead
31. child   32. back   33. lower   34. comedy
35. different   36. west   37. fall   38. arrive
39. found   40. wild   41. absence   42. permanent
43. defeat   44. public   45. friend   46. borrow
47. add   48. innocent   49. rare   50. summer

Page 71

2. more intelligent than   3. earlier than   4. more interesting than   5. wider than   6. easier than
7. more beautifully than   8. faster than   9. sooner than   10. more clearly than   11. more often than
12. better than   13. colder than   14. busier than
15. harder than   16. more carefully than   17. more often than   18. earlier than

Page 72

2. as expensive as   3. as old as   4. as well as
5. as fast as   6. as soon as   7. as well as   8. as fast as   9. as soon as   10. as cold as   11. as quickly as   12. as easily as   13. as tired as
14. as hard as   15. as good as   16. as often as
17. as rapidly as   18. as carefully as   19. as beautifully as   20. as rich as   21. as often as

Page 73

2. somewhere   3. anyone   4. any   5. some
6. anyone   7. anything   8. some   9. somewhere
10. any   11. anything   12. someone   13. anyone
14. some   15. anyone   16. any   17. somewhere

ANSWER KEY

2. 3-1st   3. 5-3rd   4. 4-2nd   5. 4-2nd   6. 4-3rd
7. 4-2nd   8. 3-1st   9. 3-1st   10. 3-1st   11. 3-2nd
12. 2-2nd   13. 5-4th   14. 3-1st   15. 2-2nd
16. 4-3rd   17. 3-2nd   18. 3-2nd   19. 2-2nd
20. 3-2nd   21. 3-2nd   22. 5-3rd   23. 2-1st

2. had taken   3. gets up   4. saw   5. have not
seen   6. has been   7. lived   8. was working
9. is knocking   10. took   11. is sleeping
12. rises   13. have not been   14. had seen
15. had not seen   16. were living   17. had finished
18. is beginning   19. is crossing   20. arrive
21. were making   22. has taught/been teaching
23. will come   24. would come   25. will see

2. to   3. on   4. for   5. for   6. around
7. from   8. from   9. against   10. on   11. to
12. in   13. by   14. on   15. for   16. of
17. on   18. at   19. at   20. on   21. for
22. at   23. in   24. behind

2. was sleeping   3. go   4. has been   5. mine
6. was   7. is waiting   8. could   9. anyone
10. than   11. an   12. a   13. live   14. were
having   15. said   16. could   17. might
18. her   19. is coming   20. are having
21. have   22. spent   23. us   24. have been

2. sang   3. rang   4. set   5. put   6. begun
7. rung   8. hurt   9. drunk   10. let   11. sunk
12. shrank   13. sprang   14. swam   15. cut
16. hit   17. spread   18. cost

2. was supposed to leave   3. am supposed to arrive
4. is supposed to be   5. are supposed to go
6. is supposed to bring   7. was supposed to
telephone   8. are supposed to write   9. is supposed
to clean   10. was supposed to arrive   11. is
supposed to be   12. was supposed to leave
13. were supposed to deliver   14. was supposed to
send   15. is supposed to be   16. is supposed to
leave   17. is supposed to stay

A. 2. used to live   3. used to be   4. used to walk
5. used to work   6. used to be   7. used to visit
8. used to go   9. used to study   10. used to be

B. 2. used to visit   3. used to play   4. used to send
5. used to write   6. used to catch   7. used to help
8. used to dance   9. used to take   10. used to walk

2. Yes, it is.-No, it isn't.   3. Yes, it did.-No, it
didn't.   4. Yes, she is.-No, she isn't.   5. Yes, we
have.-No, we haven't.   6. Yes, she can.-No, she
can't.   7. Yes, it does.-No, it doesn't.   8. Yes, he
is.-No, he isn't.   9. Yes, we have.-No, we haven't.
10. Yes, I will.-No, I won't.   11. Yes, I am.-No, I'm
not.   12. Yes, she does.-No, she doesn't.
13. Yes, I was.-No, I wasn't.   14. Yes, she was.-No,
she wasn't.

2. isn't she   3. aren't there   4. didn't you
5. won't it   6. can't she   7. wasn't it   8. hasn't he
9. isn't he   10. isn't it   11. doesn't it   12. didn't
you   13. didn't I   14. isn't she   15. hasn't she
16. isn't he   17. won't you   18. wasn't it
19. isn't he   20. haven't you

2. does it   3. is he   4. can she   5. will you
6. was it   7. have you   8. did she   9. can you
10. do you   11. does he   12. will she   13. have
you   14. has it   15. does it   16. were you
17. was she   18. has it   19. has it   20. will you

2. is it   3. isn't he   4. didn't you   5. will he
6. doesn't it   7. don't they   8. isn't she   9. won't
you   10. hasn't it   11. didn't I   12. has he
13. did he   14. doesn't she   15. haven't they
16. didn't you   17. can't she   18. didn't he
19. have you   20. didn't it   21. wasn't it
22. don't you   23. hasn't it   24. did he
25. does she

2. taking   3. investing   4. hitting   5. moving
6. eating   7. dancing   8. coming   9. hiding
10. waiting   11. speaking   12. listening
13. studying   14. using   15. painting
16. opening   17. changing   18. borrowing
19. receiving   20. making   21. working

2. leaving-to leave   3. studying-to study
4. working-to work   5. doing-to do   6. working-to
work   7. dancing-to dance   8. mentioning-to
mention   9. teaching-to teach   10. building-
to build   11. watching-to watch   12. staying-to
stay   13. criticizing-to criticize   14. finding-to find

15. speaking-to speak   16. doing-to do
17. sending-to send   18. starting-to start
19. making-to make

Page 87

2. of waiting   3. of dancing   4. on going
5. of seeing   6. about going   7. of finding
8. on speaking   9. to seeing   10. in teaching
11. in helping   12. on helping   13. of leaving
14. in learning   15. of swimming   16. in locating
17. of studying   18. of buying   19. in finding
20. for managing

Page 88

2. bitten   3. let   4. flown   5. chose   6. worn
7. fell   8. given   9. tore   10. grew   11. hid
12. known   13. driven   14. sung   15. wrote
16. blew   17. eaten   18. found   19. led
20. lain   21. thrown   22. spread   23. froze
24. spoken

Page 89

2. permanently   3. board   4. telephone
5. visit   6. come or   7. prefer   8. discuss
9. examine it   10. at the point of doing
11. discard   12. up to the present   13. accustomed
to   14. pretend   15. confused   16. by memory
17. be careful

Page 90

2. noun-verb   3. noun-verb   4. verb-noun
5. noun-verb   6. noun-verb   7. verb-noun
8. verb-noun

Page 91

3. weight   4. obligation   5. recognition
6. insistence   7. repetition   8. location
9. arrival   10. analysis   11. temptation
12. argument   13. adjustment   14. reaction
15. expectation   16. proof   17. description
18. arrangement   19. treatment   20. consideration
21. explanation   22. annoyance   23. appearance
24. belief   25. breath   26. confusion
27. inspection   28. admiration   29. relief
30. choice   31. embarrassment   32. destruction
33. completion   34. satisfaction   35. enjoyment
36. hesitation   37. paralysis   38. identification
39. protection   40. obedience   41. discovery
42. complaint   43. criticism   44. refusal

Page 92

3. to grow   4. to interfere   5. to bury   6. to
explode   7. to interrupt   8. to disturb   9. to
apologize   10. to admit   11. to repeat   12. to

prove   13. to collect   14. to relieve   15. to impress
16. to marry   17. to deny   18. to intend   19. to
choose   20. to approve   21. to advise   22. to die
23. to suspect   24. to agree   25. to amuse   26. to
excite   27. to rob   28. to succeed   29. to punish
30. to decide   31. to observe   32. to reserve
33. to adopt   34. to deceive   35. to remain
36. to lose   37. to fail   38. to warn   39. to enter
40. to begin   41. to withdraw   42. to paralyze
43. to believe   44. to conclude   45. to refuse
46. to destroy   47. to criticize   48. to complain

Page 93

2. about   3. of   4. on   5. to   6. into   7. off
8. under   9. about   10. for   11. for   12. with
13. on   14. for   15. of   16. from   17. from
18. by   19. of   20. on   21. to   22. until
23. of   24. for   25. for

Page 94

2. of moving   3. have lived   4. in learning
5. waiting   6. hearing   7. painting   8. is coming
9. cries   10. was raining   11. studying   12. is
supposed   13. me to go   14. ours   15. sunk
16. was   17. could   18. leave   19. anywhere
20. has worked   21. studied   22. were watching
23. complaining   24. Someone   25. had wanted

Page 95

2. it is   3. I was   4. I would   5. it is   6. you are
7. he was   8. she lives   9. she lived   10. I was
11. it is   12. I paid   13. he is   14. I liked
15. Adam put   16. she went   17. I put
18. we had

Page 96

2. ought to go   3. ought to choose   4. ought not to
talk   5. ought not to write   6. ought to be
7. ought to try   8. ought to get   9. ought to have
10. ought not to speak   11. ought to obey
12. ought not to read   13. ought to write
14. ought to try   15. ought to take   16. ought to
go   17. ought to be sent   18. ought to arrive
19. ought to sign   20. ought not to spend

Page 97

2. should have gone   3. should have arrived
4. should have gone   5. should have called
6. should have been sent   7. should have been
delivered   8. should have been   9. should have told
10. should have gone   11. should have read
12. should have visited   13. should have called
14. should have spent   15. should have spent
16. should have finished   17. should have been
18. should have told   19. should have asked
20. should have practiced

ANSWER KEY

PAGE 98

2. ought to have gone   3. ought to have traveled
4. ought to have saved   5. ought to have been
6. ought to have signed   7. ought to have been sent
8. ought to have arrived   9. ought to have been
delivered   10. ought to have been faxed   11. ought
to have seen   12. ought to have made   13. ought
not to have wasted   14. ought to have explained
15. ought to have telephoned   16. ought to have
worked   17. ought to have been prepared
18. ought to have telephoned   19. ought to have
gotten   20. ought to have gone   21. ought to have
written   22. ought to have been put

PAGE 99

2. works   3. hurries   4. rains   5. comes
6. attend   7. is   8. calls   9. see   10. does not
11. have   12. leave   13. gets   14. calls
15. does not   16. decide   17. gets   18. bites
19. have

PAGE 100

2. will visit   3. will miss   4. will go   5. will go
6. will learn   7. will be   8. will tell   9. will let
10. will have   11. will have   12. will be
13. will give   14. will drive   15. will take
16. will earn   17. will have   18. will explain
19. will be   20. will play

PAGE 101

2. had   3. owned   4. worked   5. knew
6. spoke   7. went   8. paid   9. knew
10. studied   11. liked   12. had   13. had
14. didn't have   15. didn't waste

PAGE 102

2. would play   3. would go   4. would speak
5. would have   6. would study   7. would go
8. would get   9. would make   10. would take
11. would go   12. would walk   13. would buy
14. would ask   15. would give   16. would stay
17. would be   18. wouldn't ride

PAGE 103

2. were   3. were   4. were   5. were   6. were
7. were   8. were   9. were   10. were   11. would
explain   12. would know   13. would go
14. would go   15. would not work   16. would not
be   17. would continue   18. would ask
19. wouldn't need

PAGE 104

2. had known   3. had called   4. had been
5. had been   6. had gone   7. had told   8. had

received   9. had had   10. had thought
11. had seen   12. had not rained   13. had left
14. had taken   15. had called   16. had known

PAGE 105

2. would have called   3. would have gone
4. would have acted   5. would have gotten
6. would have caught   7. would have refused
8. would have given   9. would have talked
10. would have gotten   11. would have done
12. would have gone   13. would have bought
14. would have taken   15. would have gone
16. would have met   17. would have driven
18. would have gone   19. would have had
20. would have been   21. would have taken
22. would have gotten

PAGE 106

2. had gone   3. spoke   4. had   5. had called
6. had studied   7. were   8. were   9. were
10. had known   11. had started   12. had studied
13. knew   14. had   15. were   16. had
17. had had   18. were   19. had been   20. were

PAGE 107

2. arrives   3. leave   4. gets   5. let   6. go
7. telephone   8. get   9. need   10. arrives
11. get   12. gets   13. see   14. gets   15. call
16. arrives   17. hear   18. comes   19. returns
20. arrives

PAGE 108

2. They live across the street from Riverside Park.
3. Sam speaks French as well as he speaks English.
4. Our teacher, Dr. Gomez, is Colombian.
5. We will celebrate New Year's Day in New York.
6. "There's a good program on TV tonight," said
Janet.   7. In Mexico, Independence Day is celebrated
in September.   8. Have you ever read the famous
Russian novel *War and Peace*?

PAGE 109

2. I studied in London, England.   3. They arrived in
Chicago, Illinois on Friday, May 3.   4. You need
eggs, flour, sugar, and milk to make a cake.   5. Beat
the eggs first, add the milk, and stir in the flour.
6. The semester ends on Friday, December 12.
7. "I'll call you later," said George.   8. Samantha
asked, "May I borrow your dictionary?"   9. We are
moving our offices to Seattle, Washington on
Monday, August 2.

PAGE 110

2. Although I was hungry all day, I didn't eat until
evening.   3. Before he got on the plane, Roger

called his office.   4. Henry cooked dinner, but he didn't wash the dishes.   5. Ann will work in the garden, and Ed will paint the fence if it doesn't rain tomorrow.   6. If I finish my homework before 8:00, I'll call you.   7. Although Carol works hard, she doesn't make a lot of money.   8. By the time we arrived, they had already left.   9. When the phone rang, I was sleeping.

PAGE 111

2. Although he was very busy, Robert offered to help Jim.   3. "This is a beautiful neighborhood," said Sara.   4. Lisa replied, "We enjoy living here very much."   5. Anil has a car, but he rarely drives it.   6. If you don't understand the lesson, ask the teacher for help.   7. My birthday is on Thursday, but we will celebrate it on Saturday.   8. John bought a ring, a bracelet, and some earrings for Mary.   9. When you get home, please walk the dog.   10. My favorite play by Shakespeare is *Romeo and Juliet*. 11. I enjoyed *Gone With the Wind*, but my sister didn't like it.   12. As soon as we get home, we'll start preparing the food for our Independence Day picnic.   13. If I had more free time, I would learn to play the piano.

PAGE 112

3. through   4. new   5. waste   6. weigh 7. week   8. would   9. night   10. no   11. sell 12. seller   13. sent   14. seen   15. fourth 16. dye   17. flower   18. rode   19. write 20. read   21. sale   22. seas/seize   23. birth 24. heel   25. here   26. seam   27. sum 28. whole   29. hire   30. hymn   31. meat 32. maid   33. male   34. inn   35. close 36. hour   37. brake   38. not   39. pare/pair 40. plain   41. peace   42. by   43. roll 44. guest   45. steel   46. sow/sew   47. sun 48. principal   49. pale   50. deer

PAGE   113

3. unable   4. unbelievable   5. irregular 6. dishonest   7. disappear   8. disobey 9. dislike   10. unattractive   11. illegible 12. mispronounce   13. disconnect   14. discontinue 15. misunderstand   16. untie   17. unwrap 18. unbutton   19. disadvantage   20. immature 21. incapable   22. disorganized   23. undress 24. unfold   25. unfortunate   26. unfair 27. disagree   28. disapprove   29. impolite 30. indiscreet   31. incorrect   32. insincere 33. uncover   34. unfurnished   35. unhealthy 36. unopened   37. unarmed   38. impatient 39. inaccurate   40. disinfect   41. disinherit 42. inconvenient   43. unreal   44. unkind 45. dissatisfied/unsatisfied   46. disagreeable 47. unpleasant   48. independent

PAGE 114

2. to   3. in   4. with   5. in   6. by   7. of 8. for   9. for   10. to   11. to   12. on   13. for 14. in   15. of   16. in   17. on   18. from 19. since   20. from   21. on   22. to   23. by 24. on   25. up/down

PAGE 115

2. I was   3. would   4. to have done   5. were 6. arrives   7. had seen   8. you live   9. theirs 10. have told   11. is ringing   12. coming 13. on waiting   14. in locating   15. is supposed 16. have you studied   17. for   18. well 19. a   20. an   21. have lived   22. comes 23. was sleeping   24. should have called   25. any

PAGE 116

2. he is, too   3. I do, too   4. his brother did, too 5. she does, too   6. I will, too   7. Ed did, too 8. she has, too   9. his sister was, too   10. they did, too   11. I am, too   12. he can, too   13. Ann has, too   14. she is, too   15. I do, too   16. his sister does, too   17. I will, too   18. you do, too 19. I may, too

PAGE 117

2. so will she   3. so have I   4. so do I   5. so can she   6. so did I   7. so will Gloria   8. so did my wife   9. so does her husband   10. so was his accomplice   11. so did I   12. so does her husband   13. so did we   14. so were the vegetables   15. so did my wife   16. so will Josie 17. so would I   18. so is my watch/mine 19. so is her husband

PAGE 118

2. Louise won't either   3. she doesn't either 4. I am/I'm not either   5. my wife doesn't either 6. I won't either   7. Rick didn't either   8. your wife won't either   9. Molly hasn't either   10. we didn't either   11. he doesn't either   12. I can't either   13. Grace isn't either   14. George can't either   15. your watch/yours doesn't either 16. Henry didn't either

PAGE 119

2. neither did the teacher   3. neither can my wife 4. neither have I   5. neither did we   6. neither could Yoko   7. neither do they   8. neither can Gail 9. neither have I   10. neither will George 11. neither did my wife   12. neither have I 13. neither is my answer/mine   14. neither do his friends   15. neither am I   16. neither did I 17. neither can Rodney   18. neither will your wife 19. neither did the teacher

ANSWER KEY

PAGE 120

2. won't 3. didn't 4. am/'m not 5. don't
6. do 7. didn't 8. didn't 9. will 10. haven't
11. has 12. can't 13. didn't 14. doesn't
15. do 16. doesn't 17. am 18. do 19. does
20. do

PAGE 121

3. pride 4. sickness 5. difference 6. simplicity
7. foolishness 8. youth 9. sadness
10. importance 11. difficulty 12. anger
13. depth 14. strength 15. height
16. nervousness 17. death 18. beauty
19. convenience 20. ugliness 21. gentleness
22. bitterness 23. possibility 24. width
25. sarcasm 26. ignorance 27. emphasis
28. strangeness 29. happiness 30. freedom
31. weakness 32. illness 33. sympathy
34. danger 35. dignity 36. absence
37. kindness 38. religion 39. truth 40. silence
41. intelligence 42. generosity 43. jealousy
44. cruelty 45. confidence 46. wealth
47. health 48. anxiety 49. mystery 50. noise

PAGE 122

3. advantageous 4. sarcastic 5. angry
6. fortunate 7. humorous 8. dignified
9. merciful 10. patient 11. energetic 12. dirty
13. absent 14. necessary 15. beautiful
16. disgraceful 17. rainy 18. wavy
19. affectionate 20. mysterious 21. suspicious
22. stylish 23. proud 24. sentimental
25. religious 26. ignorant 27. noisy 28. true
29. ambitious 30. powerful 31. silent
32. important 33. deep 34. high 35. wide
36. long 37. strong 38. cruel 39. intelligent
40. present 41. generous 42. bitter 43. dead
44. free 45. simple 46. confused 47. indifferent
48. regular

PAGE 123

2. to have been 3. to have had 4. to have
missed 5. to have worked 6. to have met
7. to have known 8. to have known 9. to have
done 10. to have seen 11. to have had 12. to
have been 13. to have arrived 14. to have done
15. to have saved 16. to have known 17. to
have been able 18. to have liked 19. to have
delivered 20. to have shown

PAGE 124

A. 2. must have come 3. must have lived
4. must have left 5. must have been 6. must have
studied 7. must have been 8. must have worked

B. 2. might have delayed 3. might have lost
4. might have forgotten 5. might have stolen
6. might have taken 7. might have called
8. might have been

PAGE 125

2. were 3. had had 4. will give 5. would have
had 6. would do 7. would go 8. would have
gone 9. see 10. will let 11. had had
12. studies 13. studied 14. had studied
15. would arrive 16. had seen 17. would work
18. had had 19. had not been 20. would not
have happened 21. had been 22. would spend

PAGE 126

2. did not go 3. ought not to tell 4. should not
have told 5. has not lived 6. were not supposed
to arrive 7. cannot speak 8. will not return
9. did not have to work 10. does not have
11. is not 12. may not park 13. were not
14. were not driving 15. would not like 16. do
not go 17. does not know 18. did not get
married 19. should not lend 20. did not arrive
21. does not listen 22. will not go 23. does not
eat 24. has not been studying 25. did not wait
26. had not left 27. did not like, neither did he/he
didn't either

PAGE 127

2. learns information about it 3. I understand it
4. cancel 5. exit 6. at 8:00 at the latest
7. immediately after 8. recover from 9. stop
trying 10. prefer to 11. return a phone call
12. more or less good 13. sometimes 14. choose
15. postpone 16. consider 17. recently